Profiles
in
Investigative
Journalism

---

by
ELIZABETH LEVY

FOUR WINDS PRESS
NEW YORK

Library of Congress Cataloging in Publication Data

Levy, Elizabeth.
  By-lines: profiles in investigative journalism.

  SUMMARY: Discusses the characteristics of investigative jour-
nalism as exemplified in the work of seven journalists: Selwyn
Raab, Edward R. Murrow, I. F. Stone, Oriana Fallaci, Robert
Woodward and Carl Bernstein, and Gail Sheehy.
  1. Journalists—United States—Juvenile literature.
[1. Journalists. 2. Journalism] I. Title.
PN4871.L37   070′.92′2   75–15930
ISBN 0–590–17391–X

PUBLISHED BY FOUR WINDS PRESS

A DIVISION OF SCHOLASTIC MAGAZINES, INC., NEW YORK, N.Y.

COYPRIGHT © 1975 BY ELIZABETH LEVY

PRINTED IN THE UNITED STATES OF AMERICA

LIBRARY OF CONGRESS CATALOG CARD NUMBER: 75–15930

1 2 3 4 5   79 78 77 76 75

Contents

Introduction

What is an investigative reporter? What do reporters do, if not investigate stories? In an age when people are accustomed to succinct sixty-second television news stories, the word "investigate" has been coined to describe the handful of men and women who go beyond the obvious aspects of the story. For example, if a fire broke out in your block, one reporter might describe the fire itself and the damage it caused, interview you and your neighbors about how frightened you were, perhaps interview the firemen about the danger, then go back and write a story. Another reporter might try to find out who owned the building. Was it well kept? Did the owner have any reason to want to get rid of the building The second reporter would be investigating.

It might turn out that the fire was an accident, and that all those extra questions led nowhere. Investigative reporters waste a lot of time on stories that don't lead anywhere. It's expensive to keep investigative reporters on salary. Sometimes good reporters work for months on a lead and come up with nothing.

In the last decade, another phrase has cropped up to describe journalism today. It is vaguely referred to as "new journalism." In one sense, the new journalists are similar to investigative reporters in that they ask more questions than the run-of-the-mill journalists. But the new journalists are asking different questions. A new journalist covering a fire would ask, "How does it feel to be a reporter at a scene of disaster and stick my notebook into the faces of people who have just lost their homes?" New journalists turn the table on a reporter's traditional job, and they ask questions of themselves. They argue that only by including their own feelings and sensitivities in the story can the reader get a full picture of what really happened.

When Oriana Fallaci, an Italian journalist who is described in Chapter 2, writes about astronauts, she includes whether or not she daydreamed while they were talking to her, and even what she daydreamed about. She and the other new journalists believe that the meaning of a subject is complete if it includes what the person viewing the story felt at the time.

Some commentators have differentiated new journalists from traditional journalists by declaring that the new journalists have lost their objectivity. Objectivity is the ability to let the facts stand on their own. The objective reporter carefully avoids inserting his or her own opinions. The new journalists argue that for a reporter to write an "objective" story when he feels the truth to be something different is a lie. Edward R. Murrow, as you will see in Chapter 4, when confronted with an obvious miscarriage of justice, said, "We simply can't do an 'on the other hand' on this." Murrow is certainly not considered a new journalist, but he felt that there may not always be two equal sides to every question.

All reporters have to rely on facts. A good reporter, whether new or traditional, is not the same as a good editorialist. An editorialist uses the force and eloquence of argument to convert people to his or her point of view. A reporter, investigative, new, or traditional has to tell the story through facts.

However, each reporter has to decide where to go to look for facts. It is here that the new journalists are right in claiming that no reporter is objective. There are simply too many stories to cover. All reporters have to make a choice, and in making that choice a reporter exercises some personal preference.

In writing about journalists, I have had to make a choice. My choice shows that I am not an "objective" observer. When I looked over my selections, I discovered that the people I had chosen had several characteristics in common, and that these were characteristics that I admire. The first characteristic isn't usually considered a virtue.

DISTRUSTFUL

A number of words describe this state of mind: cynical, suspicious, nongullible, distrustful. Whichever you prefer, the fact is that the men and women in this book do not believe much, until and unless, they have been able to verify it for themselves. They share a basic distrust about what people say—and the more powerful the people, the greater the skepticism. Given the choice between accepting something at face value or suspecting its accuracy, our reporters opt for suspicion every time.

"The thing you've got to remember," says I. F. Stone, the subject of Chapter 5, "is all governments are liars."

When Bob Woodward heard the Republicans claim that Cuban patriots had broken into Democratic headquarters at the Watergate complex, he commented, "It had an aroma, if not a stink, about it."

When Selwyn Raab investigated the case of George Whitmore, who was accused of rape and murder, he felt "something smelled. . . . There was something smelly about it."

When Oriana Fallaci interviewed Henry Kissinger, and he denied that he had any fascination with power, she simply didn't believe him. She kept probing.

What is so astonishing is that in each of these cases, practically every other reporter, working on the same story, did not have the same reaction. I. F. Stone was the only reporter who did not believe the government's account of the Tonkin Gulf incident. Selwyn Raab spent a very long time being the only reporter who didn't believe George Whitmore guilty. Woodward and Bernstein and their paper, *The Washington Post*, were almost alone in believing that the Watergate story was bigger than it appeared on the surface. Oriana Fallaci was the only reporter to pierce the seemingly impenetrable surface of a man who had become a symbol of enigmatic power to most reporters.

When each of these individuals is asked to accept a given event or personality, something inside him or her says, "I don't believe you."

NERVE

Columnist Mary McGrory was once asked what it took to be an investigative reporter. "It's a gift," she said. "A lot of people don't have the stomach for it. They don't have the will for it. They don't have the brass it takes to go up to a total stranger, take him by the collar and say, 'Now you tell me. . . .' It's not everybody that can do it. I can't, for instance."

The reporters who are included in this book have a lot of nerve. They seem to have a built-in need in their systems to go out on a limb for their story. Some kind of adrenalin starts pumping in the face of adversity to make them do an even better job of investigating than they might otherwise have done.

It takes a lot of nerve to be a good reporter. If you print a story that disturbs the accepted view of something, many people are going to be angry and hurt. Most of the reporters in this book admit that they have moments when they say to themselves, "What if I'm really wrong? What if I've somehow concocted this story out of nothing? What if it doesn't hang together the way I'm telling it?"

Usually, they quickly answer those doubts with, "I can't be wrong. I've gotten the facts on this and they add up. Now, I'm going to dig even deeper to prove I'm right."

CONVICTIONS

The best reporters are not necessarily objective truth-seekers. The men and women in this book have definite opinions as to what is right and what is wrong. Without this ability to make judgments, they would never be able to suspect that "something is wrong" with the official story.

Edward R. Murrow, for example, was willing to undertake an examination of Joseph McCarthy at a time when other reporters were unwilling to risk their career on such a controversial subject. It was his opinion that McCarthyism was ruining the lives of innocent people, and Murrow felt he had to expose McCarthyism for what it was.

I. F. Stone has strong beliefs and opinions about government. He not only believes that all governments are liars, but that our government is basically unfair.

The fact that the people in this book hold strong opinions does not mean that they allowed their opinions to interfere with the accuracy of their investigations. My point is that their opinions give them an edge. That edge enables them to believe less than anyone else, dig deeper than anyone else, and somehow sustain themselves through a great deal of criticism and controversy. People who do not allow themselves to have strong opinions (or reporters who have talked themselves into thinking it is wrong to even admit having them) do not make good investigators. There is no fuel to feed the fire.

If, as I claim, the best reporters are often those with strong opinions, we have to consider another essential ingredient in good journalism. It has nothing to do with the personality of the journalist; it has to do with the freedom to investigate.

Freedom of the press is basically freedom of opinion. Being free to believe anything one wished would be meaningless if that freedom did not extend to putting that belief down on paper. The writers of the American constitution knew they were taking a risk when they made freedom of the press an absolute. They knew from experience that freedom of the press meant a risk to the government in power, but they felt that freedom was worth the risk.

In fact, putting ideas down on paper was probably one of the causes of the American revolution. The most opinionated American reporter was probably that slightly mad troublemaker, Tom Paine.

Arriving in the colonies at the end of 1775, Paine had already developed strong opinions on what the situation was here. Monarchy was abhorrent, George III the worst monarch of all, and revolution the only answer. Taking up his pen, Paine wrote a pamphlet called *Common Sense*, in which he laid out a tight case for independence, exposing George III as the "royal brute of Great Britain." Paine cited the benefits that would come to an independent America. He closed saying, "Freedom hath been shunted around the globe. Asia and Africa have long expelled her. Europe regards her like a stranger, and England hath given her warning to depart. O receive the fugitive and prepare in time an asylum for mankind!"

Circulation of the paper was enormous, and literally thousands of colonists caught the revolutionary fever from the words of Tom Paine.

Paine was never jailed for writing *Common Sense*, though his action was certainly advocating rebellion, and the king's soldiers would have locked him up if the American revolution hadn't interfered.

The original constitution did not include freedom of the press. However, many people realized that the revolution might never have happened if men like Tom Paine and Sam Adams had not had the courage to write, even if it meant possible imprisonment. The founding fathers discovered that they would not be able to get their constitution ratified unless they granted a bill of rights including absolute freedom of the press. The First Amendment states that "Congress shall make no law . . . abridging the freedom of speech of the press."

There is nothing ambiguous about those words. Congress is forbidden to make any law that restricts freedom of the press. Almost no other country has followed our example and granted complete freedom of the press. It didn't take very long for some people in America to regret that the First Amendment had ever been written.

In the twenty years after the establishment of the nation, newspapers became political organs supporting one party or the other. There was so much name calling and so many vicious attacks on politicians by their opponents, that soon people began to argue that complete freedom of the press wasn't such a good idea after all.

The Federalists, who controlled the government in 1798, passed a sedition act which made it a crime to write anything "false, scandalous or malicious" against the government. These are very vague words. Several editors were put in jail over the next few years. It became clear that the government could interpret the word "malicious" to its own advantage. Nothing could be printed if it displeased the authority in power. The name calling might have been annoying, and even a little frightening, but the suppression of the press was even worse. In 1801, when Thomas Jefferson took office, the alien and sedition laws were not renewed.

Congress learned its lesson well. For the next 117 years, no further attempt was made to limit what journalists might or might not say.

Just at the beginning of the twentieth century, a new kind of journalist began to appear. This journalist was not interested in just describing events. Nor was this journalist a political hack like the journalists in the 1700s.

These journalists were called "the muckrakers" because they raked around in the muck and the underside of different aspects of American life. Their object was not to titillate their audience. They wanted reform. Gail Sheehy is a modern reporter in the muckraking tradition. Her exposé on prostitution revealed that many "respectable" landlords were making money off prostitution. Her articles caused such a furor that the mayor of New York began a clean-up campaign against the prostitution hotels and their landlords.

There seems to be a resurgence of muckraking in recent years. The last time reporters were as influential as they are today was in the 1900s. At that time the muckraking reporters were at the forefront of a wave of reform that hit many aspects of American life. Upton Sinclair wrote about the filthy conditions of the Chicago meat market, and laws were passed to have meat inspected by the federal government. Ida Tarbell exposed the tremendous power of Standard Oil, and new laws were passed limiting the power of the huge trusts. Lincoln Steffens wrote a series exposing the evils and corruption in city governments, and many progressive reforms were passed. Journalists gained a new respect, and new power. No sooner did they expose a story, then it seemed as if a law was passed to correct the condition.

Then in 1918, when America became involved in

its first serious battle with overseas enemies, Congress passed the Espionage Act, which prohibited writing anything that might interfere with the war effort. But how was the law to be interpreted? Was there any way to draw the line between threats to national security and legitimate government criticism? Justice Oliver Wendell Holmes ruled that the press could only be limited if the "words used . . . are of such a nature as to create a clear and present danger that will bring about the substantive evils that Congress has a right to prevent."

This meant that the burden was on the government to prove a "clear and present danger." In 1972, for example, President Nixon instructed the attorney general to seek a court injunction to prevent *The Washington Post* and *The New York Times* from publishing the Pentagon papers because the government said its national security was in "clear and present danger." The Supreme Court ruled that since the Pentagon papers dealt with the past there was no clear and present danger to foreign policy.

Apart from the ever changing statutes on obscenity —which do not apply to the work of most reporters— the only other enforceable legal limits are the laws governing libel and slander.

In 1963, in a landmark decision on *Sullivan v. New York Times*, the Supreme Court ruled that in cases involving public officials, no reporter or paper could be held libel for printing falsehoods if such falsehoods were the result of carelessness. If the reporter had meant to be malicious, then both the reporter and the paper were guilty of libel.

Debate still rages over this decision. Many argue that the Sullivan decision has given reporters freedom to print whatever lies they want. Reporters no longer have to worry about being sued if they report something someone tells them and it turns out to be a lie.

Many journalists give the Sullivan decision credit for encouraging healthy and much needed criticism of government and politics in this country. They point out that the Sullivan rule pertains only to public officials and the ordinary citizen's privacy is still protected.

There is one last potential "legal" limitation that hangs over the heads of reporters and that concerns the right of a reporter to protect his source of information. It is only a potential limit because so far the courts have not ruled definitely on whether or not a reporter can be ordered to tell the names of informants. One cannot read about Woodward and Bernstein's detecting of the Watergate story without concluding that unless they had been able to guarantee their sources complete anonymity and secrecy, there might never have been accurate reporting of the Watergate break-in.

The law about whether or not a reporter has a right to "shield" sources is particularly murky. In 1972, the Supreme Court ruled that reporters had no protection

under the First Amendment against grand jury questions. However, the Supreme Court split 5–4 on that
decision, and the majority opinion made it clear that
their decision was to apply in this one particular case,
and was not to be taken as a general rule.

At this time, twenty-five states have "shield laws"
which allow reporters the right to protect confidential
sources, but several times local judges have ruled that
these laws do not apply to the particular information
wanted. There have been many efforts to get Congress
to enact federal legislation to protect reporters' sources,
but so far these efforts have not been successful.

So much for the legal forces that influence reporters.
What other demands or limitations are placed upon the
journalist's freedom to question, to search, and then to
print. One obvious constriction is the philosophy and
judgment of the management of either the newspaper
or the television station.

Two of the reporters you will meet in this book don't
have a problem with management. I. F. Stone put out
his own paper. He could say and do exactly what he
pleased. Similarly, Oriana Fallaci sells most of her
stories to whomever will print them, and because she is
good, her stories sell. But Fallaci and Stone are excep-
tions. They are basically free-lancers and write what
they want. The rest of the reporters in this book work
for others.

When you read the chapter on Selwyn Raab, you will see that because his editor did not agree with him, Raab's stories got placed on the back and middle pages of the paper without pictures. Woodward and Bernstein had numerous meetings with the editors of their paper to go over their story. They were blessed with a courageous publisher and editor.

Even Edward R. Murrow, who was so esteemed he was given virtually a free hand by CBS, felt he had to call his network executives when he was going to air an extremely controversial program.

In short, the views of stockholders, subscribers, and advertisers *do* matter to the managers of the news media and ultimately they matter to the reporter.

Fortunately, the news business is also highly competitive, and a story that hits sensitive nerves will probably sell a lot of newspapers or attract a lot of people to watch a television program. The combination of legal freedom and the competitive nature of the news business has made American reporting the best in the world. Remarkably few reporters complain of being called off a good story. In fact, most editors complain that there are too few first-rate investigative reporters to go around. Here, then, are some investigative reporters who I consider first-rate, and who have earned the respect of their readers and colleagues.

1

Woodward and Bernstein:

Catching the Dinosaur's Tail

Robert Woodward and Carl Bernstein are the young reporters who came up with the first hard news that tied the Watergate burglars to the Nixon administration. When the Watergate story broke, Woodward and Bernstein were two unknown reporters for *The Washington Post*. Out of the hundreds of reporters who cover Washington, scarcely more than a dozen were assigned to Watergate in the beginning, and only Woodward and Bernstein followed up on the story. All through the summer of 1972, Woodward and Bernstein put in long hours slowly piecing together the complicated Watergate story. As Brendan Gill said on television's *Behind the Lines*, "They grasped the tip of the tail of what seemed to be a nasty little local rat, and it turned into an immense crooked-minded dinosaur."

Woodward and Bernstein—today it is impossible to

think of one without thinking of the other, but back before Watergate, the two didn't even like each other, much less think of themselves as a team. Woodward was twenty-nine. Bernstein was twenty-eight. They had never worked together before. Woodward is neat, very much upperclass, a son of a Republican judge, a graduate of Yale University. Bernstein is Jewish, a college dropout, and sloppy.

Woodward began his reporting career on a local Maryland newspaper, but his ambition was to work for a major Washington newspaper on important stories. He called the editor of *The Washington Post* and asked for a job. When told there were no openings, Woodward started calling every week to find out if there was any hope. Finally, the editor told him to quit pestering him. Then the editor went on vacation. Woodward called him at home to find out if the situation had changed, and if maybe a job was available. The editor was furious. He couldn't believe Woodward would have the gall to call a man on vacation and bug him for a job. The editor slammed the receiver down, hanging up on Woodward, muttering to his wife about the nerve of some guys. "But isn't this just the kind of reporter you're always saying you want?" asked the editor's wife.

The editor decided she was right and hired Woodward, who went to work bothering other people with his insistent phone calls. On his first day of work, Woodward made close to a hundred phone calls looking for a story. He won a reputation as a hard worker, but a terrible writer. One of the jokes around the newsroom was that "English was not Woodward's native language."

Carl Bernstein started out in the newspaper business when he was only sixteen, working as a copy boy. He became a full-time reporter at age nineteen. Bernstein was a good writer, but he had a reputation for pushing himself onto other people's stories, and sometimes stealing by-lines right out from under the people who felt they deserved them.

On Saturday June 18, 1972, Woodward was assigned to cover the story of a break-in at the Democratic National Committee Headquarters at Watergate. At this point, Watergate was thought to be merely a local crime story. Several suspects had been caught in the act of breaking and entering. The suspects all wore playtex rubber surgical gloves. The police found walkie-talkies, 50 rolls of unexposed film, lock picks, pen-size teargas guns, and bugging devices. Several of the suspects had large amounts of cash on them, mostly in one hundred dollar bills with their serial numbers in sequence.

Woodward realized right away that this was not an ordinary story. "There are fifty burglaries a day in

Washington," Woodward told a reporter, and "there had never been one like that. Men in business suits, hundred dollar bills, sophisticated electronic and photographic equipment. It had an aroma if not a stink about it immediately, and that's not just from the privileged position of today. When we looked at it then, we were incredulous and said, "My god, there must be something there."

Woodward went down to the courthouse for the preliminary hearing of the suspects. He sat in the front row. The judge asked James McCord, one of the suspects, what he did for a living. McCord mumbled in a very low voice that he was a security consultant who used to work for the CIA. Because Woodward was in the front row, he was one of the few reporters to hear this first hint of a link between the Watergate burglary and the CIA.

Woodward rushed back to the newsroom to write his story. When he got there he found Carl Bernstein hanging around the editor's desk. Bernstein was officially assigned to the Virginia politics desk, and had no legitimate reason for being involved in the Watergate story. Bernstein was trying to muscle in on Woodward's story. Not only trying but succeeding. Bernstein had talked the editor into letting him write profiles of the seven suspects.

The next day, *The Washington Post* put the Watergate story on the front page. *The New York Times* carried it on page twenty-eight. This pattern would keep up for months. While other newspapers virtually ignored Watergate, *The Post* kept after the story and eventually assigned Woodward and Bernstein to work on it full time.

"Neither the editors, the publishers, nor ourselves had any preconceived notion about where the story was going to go," Bernstein told a reporter. "If it went nowhere, it went nowhere, but they made the commitment to find out where it was going to go and wherever the chips fell they were going to go with it."

The first day after the Watergate break-in, Woodward had worked on the story from nine in the morning until eight at night. As he left he had a feeling that he should stay longer to try to track down more information about James McCord.

When Woodward came in the next morning, he wanted to kick himself for not listening to his instinct. There was an item on the *Associated Press* wire that showed that James McCord had once worked for the Committee to Re-Elect the President, President Nixon's campaign organization, headed by former Attorney General John Mitchell. The fact that James McCord was tied in with the President's election campaign was a much bigger "scoop" than Woodward's story of the fact that McCord used to work for the CIA.

In the American press, competition for getting the story first is a constant pressure on reporters. This is particularly true for a daily newspaper, and nowhere is there more competition than in Washington. Washington probably has more reporters *per capita* than any other city. Reporters are constantly running into each other in their search for stories. A few hours' head start on an important story can mean the difference between success and failure for a reporter. Woodward was clearly one of the most competitve reporters to come on the Washington scene in quite a while. He had made up his mind not to be "scooped" again if he could help it, even if it meant working night and day.

That day John Mitchell issued a statement that James McCord was merely a consultant who once worked part time for the Committee to Re-Elect the President. Mitchell said McCord had been hired to make sure that nobody was bugging the Republicans' phones. Mitchell went on to say, "We want to emphasize that this man and the other people involved were not operating either on our behalf or with our consent. There is no place in our campaign or in the electoral process for this type of activity and we will not permit or condone it."

Woodward went straight to work trying to find more information about exactly what James McCord did. No one answered at either McCord's home or his place

of business. Woodward realized there were a lot of phone calls to make if he wanted to find out anything, more than enough work for two. He got Bernstein to help him. They sat down with a phone directory which lists phone numbers by street address. Then they compiled a list of all the tenants in the building where McCord had his security consultant office, and started calling every name on the list, hoping that someone would be able to tell them something about McCord.

It is not easy for most people to make phone calls to strangers and force yourself upon them. Throughout the Watergate story, Woodward and Bernstein spent an incredible amount of time in the sheer drudgery of making phone call after phone call. Most of their calls yielded nothing that would help.

Finally, one person vaguely remembered that a teenage girl who had worked for him part time had said her father knew James McCord. It wasn't much of a clue. The man couldn't even remember the girl's first name, only her last name, Westall. Woodward and Bernstein went back to their phone books and started calling every Westall in the Washington area. The fifth one admitted knowing James McCord.

Woodward and Bernstein identified themselves as reporters from *The Washington Post*. *The Post* has a firm rule that it will not print a story if the person being interviewed does not know he or she is talking to a reporter.

However, after the reporter has identified himself, *The Post* allows him quite a bit of freedom in order to get a story. For example, James McCord's friend did not realize that McCord had been arrested. Woodward lied about why he was calling. He told Westall he was gathering background material for a possible profile on McCord as a security consultant.

Westall was not used to talking to the press. He seemed flattered that a reporter would want to talk to him about his friend James McCord. He told Woodward that McCord was a "good family man, a man to be trusted, hardworking," and so forth. Then, Mr. Westall casually dropped the news that James McCord worked *full time* for John Mitchell's Committee to Re-Elect the President.

Woodward hung up the phone greatly excited. The Watergate story was scarcely more than twenty-four hours old, and he had caught the administration in the first outright lie of what would become known as the "cover-up." John Mitchell had definitely said that McCord had only worked for the Committee part time.

As soon as he got off the phone, Woodward began banging out his story on the typewriter. In the book *All the President's Men*, Woodward described in the third person what happened next. "As he finished one paragraph he handed it to the editor, and he couldn't help noticing that the editor passed his copy to Bernstein. Woodward was annoyed. This was just the kind of horning in he was afraid of. Then, he read what Bernstein had done with his copy and realized Bernstein really was a better writer than he."

Woodward and Bernstein began working together full time. Their next big break came from a tip from the police. The address book of one of the suspects contained the name of Howard Hunt with the small notation, "W. House, " and "W. H." beside it.

Woodward called Howard Hunt at the White House and when he told Hunt his name was in an address book found on the Watergate burglars, Hunt swore and hung up. Later Woodward found out that Howard Hunt had been with the CIA.

Woodward and Bernstein couldn't believe the story they were unraveling. It was still only two days after the original break-in, and now Watergate was tied in twice to the CIA, had a direct tie to President Nixon's re-election campaign, and had at least a tenuous link to the White House itself. Woodward wrote a story whose headline read, "White House Consultant Linked to Bugging Suspects."

On the same day that story was printed, Ron Ziegler, White House press secretary, read a statement expressing the views of the president that "Watergate was a third-rate burglary attempt not worthy of further notice."

Woodward and Bernstein were both convinced that

they were onto the story of their lives, but suddenly it seemed to go dead. Howard Hunt disappeared and nobody could find him. Woodward and Bernstein made hundreds and hundreds of phone calls. They called people at the FBI, people who worked at the White House, people who worked for the Committee to Re-Elect the President, but they could get no further news. They could find nothing about who the Watergate burglars had been working for and what they were after. Bernstein kept getting lots of hints that Watergate could "explode" dangerously close to the White House, but almost all the information he received was hearsay and rumors. Nobody could tell him anything that *The Post* could print.

Woodward and Bernstein had been working on the Watergate story for ten days and they had come up with nothing. On a daily paper, ten days is a long time to spend on one story, especially if the result is zero lines of print. A paper has to come out every day. There's a lot of news to be covered, and a lot of pages to be filled.

It was an election year and *The Post* needed Woodward and Bernstein to cover other stories. As the Watergate story seemed to die, the editors began to feel that Woodward and Bernstein should get back to stories that *The Post* could print.

Woodward and Bernstein felt their editors were

making a big mistake. Bernstein wrote a five page memo outlining all the hints he and Woodward had picked up indicating that Watergate was a big story. The next day, the editors at *The Post* decided to let Woodward and Bernstein continue on the story full time.

It was June 27, 1972. That afternoon, President Nixon made his first public announcement concerning Watergate. "The White House has no involvement whatsoever in this particular incident."

Woodward and Bernstein's primary job now became tracking down all the misleading "leaks" that were coming out of the White House and the Committee to Re-Elect the President. Most of these leaks suggested that the Watergate break-in had been organized and paid for by Cuban refugees who wanted to prove that the Democrats were taking money from Fidel Castro.

This was the cover-up story that was later discovered to have been fabricated by the people close to President Nixon in order to explain the Watergate break-in. Woodward and Bernstein knew the Watergate burglars were tied to the Committee to Re-Elect the President in some way. Their hardest job was to try to find someone on the president's campaign staff to talk to them. However, ever since the Watergate break-in, the people who worked at the Committee to Re-Elect the President had been acting as if they were an army under siege. A uniformed guard stood at the entrance, escorting visitors to and from their appointments. Even the Committee's telephone directory was considered a classified document.

A woman gave Woodward and Bernstein a copy of the telephone directory and told them she would lose her job if it was discovered she had let the reporters see the Committee's telephone directory.

Woodward and Bernstein were thrilled to finally get at least a tiny bit of their story down on paper. Up until now, all the information they had came from rumors or people talking to them. The telephone directory was the first concrete evidence that they had of the inside workings of the Committee. Woodward and Bernstein wrote that they studied the directory as if they were gypsies reading tea leaves.

They used the directory to figure out who worked for whom and who held positions of responsibility. Who was it that had given the money out to the Watergate burglars? Who had ordered the burglary in the first place? Why?

Woodward and Bernstein knew that employees of the Committee to Re-Elect the President would not feel free to talk to them in their offices. Therefore, rather than try to reach anybody who worked for the Committee during the day, Woodward and Bernstein went out in the evening to visit the homes of employees of the Committee.

By now, Woodward and Bernstein had stopped

being suspicious of each other and had begun to appreciate each other's strengths. The Wategate story was so vague and hard to grasp that each felt relieved that he wasn't working on it alone. It helped to have somebody to talk over the bits of information. It was like working a jigsaw puzzle with a friend. One reporter alone would have felt overwhelmed.

Nowhere was the gathering of details more frustrating than when they tried to see people who worked at the Committee. Moreover, nowhere is there a better example of the type of hard work that investigative journalism requires. Woodward and Bernstein worked a full day at *The Post*, and then every night they would show up on someone's doorstep, usually someone who didn't want to talk to them.

Woodward and Bernstein always identified themselves as reporters, but by their own admission, after that they were less truthful. Frequently they lied and told the person they were visiting, "Someone at the Committee told us you were disturbed by some of the things going on there and you would be a good person to talk to." In actuality, Woodward and Bernstein had gotten the person's name from their precious phone directory, but they claimed that they couldn't say who had given them the person's name because they were protecting confidential sources. This ruse had the double advantage of covering up the reporter's lie as well as reassuring the person that what he said would be kept confidential.

Once Bernstein called on a woman whom he knew was in a position to give him information. The woman refused to talk to him. Just as the door was about to shut in his face, Bernstein noticed a pack of cigarettes on a table in the hall. He asked for one, and when the woman agreed, Bernstein stepped into the hall and took one. He had gotten himself inside. Then he asked if he could sit down and finish the cigarette. He dragged on the cigarette slowly, anything to prolong his visit. Eventually the woman began to feel comfortable with Bernstein and gave him some information.

One of Woodward and Bernstein's basic techniques was to always act as if they had more information than they did. This is a technique employed by many good reporters. Most people feel free to talk about confidential matters if they think you already have the information. Then the person being interviewed feels as if they are just filling in a few details.

Several committee employees told Woodward and Bernstein about widespread destruction of records immediately after the Watergate break-in. Others mentioned large sums of money being passed around mysteriously. Gradually a pattern started to emerge. Because the Watergate cover-up was so vague, *The Post* did not want to publish anything unless they could be

absolutely sure they were not printing rumor. Woodward and Bernstein and their editors had worked out a
rule not to print any information unless it could be
confirmed by two independent sources.

Bernstein and Woodward found the lack of concrete
information frustrating. They had many clues that
Watergate had been directed by the Republicans and
that Republicans in the circle close to the President
had been lying, but they needed help in sorting out
their information. They needed to know what information was on the right track and what was completely
out of line.

Woodward had a friend who was high up in the
executive branch of the government, and who was not
happy with the way things were being handled at the
White House. He agreed to help Woodward untangle
some of the confusion surrounding the Watergate
cover, but only if Woodward promised never to quote
him directly, even as an anonymous source. Often
someone will tell a reporter something, but insist that
they not be quoted by name. Then you might read in
the paper "informed sources" or "our sources tell us"
or "a high administration official," but the official is
never named.

However, sometimes a source is worried that even
if they are quoted anonymously, someone will know
they talked because only one person could have that
information. Then the source will say you can't quote

me at all, you can't even use the information I give you, but if you get the information from one other source, I'll tell you whether or not the story is true. In newspaper jargon this type of discussion is called "deep background." Woodward's editor started calling Woodward's source "Deep Throat," the title of a popular pornographic movie. The name stuck.

In the beginning, Deep Throat would chat with Woodward over the telephone, but after a couple of weeks, Deep Throat said it was too dangerous even to talk on the phone. However, Deep Throat agreed to meet Woodward whenever Woodward felt he needed him. If Woodward wanted a meeting, he would take a flower pot with a red cloth flag hanging from it and move it from the front of his apartment's balcony to the back. Deep Throat drove past Woodward's apartment every day to see if the signal was up. If it was, Deep Throat would meet Woodward at two in the morning in an underground parking garage.

Deep Throat helped to confirm much of the information Woodward and Bernstein had gathered. In early October, *The Post* published an article by Woodward and Bernstein stating that the Watergate operation had been controlled by several top people close to John Mitchell and that the Committee had a special fund of $300,000 for sensitive political projects. Then Woodward and Bernstein found someone at the Committee who said that John Mitchell himself had controlled the fund that had paid for the Watergate burglaries. Deep Throat confirmed the information.

It is important to recall this was taking place *before* the election of 1972. John Mitchell was one of the most powerful men in the country. President Nixon was about to be re-elected by a huge majority. Only Massachusetts and the District of Columbia would vote against him. Watergate was not a household word. Nobody even breathed the word "impeachment." Fewer than 50 percent of the people in the country had even heard of the Watergate break-in, and most of that 50 percent didn't think it was important. When Woodward and Bernstein wrote that Watergate had been controlled by President Nixon's former attorney general, they were taking a great risk.

Woodward and Bernstein say they always had the horrifying thought, "What if we are wrong?" There was always the terrifying possibility that they were being set up. The night before they were going to publish the big story about Mitchell, Bernstein called Mitchell in New York. It was around 11:30 p.m. Bernstein took careful notes of everything that was said.

Bernstein: Sir, I'm sorry to bother you at this hour, but we are running a story in tomorrow's paper that in effect says you controlled secret funds at the Committee while you were attorney general.

Mitchell: Jeeeeeeesus, you said that. What does it say?

Bernstein: I'll read you the first few paragraphs. . . .

Mitchell: All that's crap. It's all been denied. Katie Graham (publisher of *The Post*) is going to get her—caught in a big fat wringer if that's published. Good Christ! That's the most sickening thing I've ever heard. We're going to do a story on all of you.

When Bernstein hung up after his phone call with Mitchell, he realized for the first time that Mitchell was flesh and blood.

"(My) skin felt prickly . . . through the use of the neutral language of a reporter's trade, (we) had called John Mitchell a crook. I did not savor the moment. His (Mitchell's) tone was so filled with hate and loathing that (I) felt threatened. (I) was shocked at Mitchell's language, his ugliness. *'We're going to do a story on all of you . . .'* Once the election was over they could do almost anything they damn well pleased. And get away with it."

Katherine Graham, publisher of *The Washington Post*, told a reporter for *New York Magazine*, "I've lived with White House anger before, but I've never seen anything that achieved this kind of fury and heat." However, she says she never considered telling Woodward and Bernstein to stop publishing their stories.

After the publication of the story about John Mitchell, Ron Ziegler, White House press secretary, and others in the Nixon administration began a series of attacks on *The Post*, accusing Woodward and Bernstein of employing hypocrisy, shabby journalism, character assassination, and guilt by association.

In many newspapers across the country, the White House denials of Woodward and Bernstein's stories made bigger headlines than the stories themselves. However, the fact that President Nixon and others at the White House were so defensive about Woodward and Bernstein's stories made other reporters and editors suspect that Wategate might be bigger than the administration claimed.

In December 1972, the original seven Watergate defendants were tried in Judge Sirica's courtroom. They pleaded guilty. During the trial, Judge Sirica, who had a reputation for being a demanding judge, made it clear that he had "not been satisfied that all pertinent facts that might be available . . . have been produced." He assigned the defendants to particularly hard sentences for the felony of breaking and entering, giving the leaders, James McCord and Gordon Liddy, fifteen years. Sirica said that if any defendants coop-

erated by telling the court who had been really responsible for hiring them, he might lighten the sentences.

In March 1973, Watergate burglar James McCord
wrote a letter to Judge Sirica saying that he and the
other Watergate suspects had been paid to keep silent
and had been asked to perjure themselves by people
high up in the Nixon administration. Now reporters
swarmed all over the Watergate cover-up story. President Nixon's top aides resigned. White House press
secretary Ron Ziegler personally apologized for accusing *The Post* of shabby journalism.

Woodward and Bernstein won the Pulitzer Prize
for their reporting. Suddenly these two young men
became a power in Washington. Almost everyone
wanted to call them and tell their own version of what
was going on. Instead of having to go out at all hours
of the night, stories were walking in the front door.

Watergate made Woodward and Bernstein two of
the most famous reporters in the country. A movie is
being made about them; their book became a best-
seller. No one can tell how their fame will affect their
work. They are both still working for *The Washington
Post*. They are writing a book about the last 100 days
of President Nixon's administration. It's unlikely that
a story like Watergate will happen to them again, but
the tale of how they broke the Watergate story will
remain a classic in American journalism.

2

Oriana Fallaci:

Inner and Outer Journeys

Oriana Fallaci was born in Florence, Italy, in 1930. Her father was a liberal who fought Mussolini's rise to power. When Mussolini made a pact with Hitler, Fallaci's father joined the underground. By the time of World War II, Fallaci was ten years old, and she fought the Nazis in the underground herself, joining the Corps of Volunteers for Freedom. When the Nazis occupied Florence, her father was jailed and tortured, but he was finally released alive.

After the war Oriana Fallaci thought she wanted to be a doctor, but at sixteen she discovered the power of words, and decided to become a writer. "I sat at the typewriter for the first time and fell in love with the words that emerged like drops, one by one, and remained on the white sheet of paper . . . every drop became something that if spoken would have flown away, but on the sheets as words, became solidified, whether they were good or bad."

When you read Oriana Fallaci's journalism, you become aware that she loves words. It is this love of words that sets her somewhere in the middle between reporter and novelist. Often she includes everything in her reporting: how she feels, what irritates her, what moves her. She likes to speculate on how all the influences and sights and sounds in her life tie together. In short, her writing exemplifies all the qualities associated with "new journalism."

"I do not believe in objectivity," she writes. "As far as I know objectivity exists only in mathematics where two plus two makes four, period. Within conscience or memory, objectivity cannot exist, and to demand it would be grotestque. A true portrait of a man cannot be achieved without the beliefs, the feelings, the tastes of the painter.

However, just as the best abstract artists are capable of drawing a detailed picture of a real subject, Fallaci is first a reporter after facts. She is known as a superb interviewer; in fact, among journalists, a new verb has been coined in her honor—to be "Fallaci-ed."

In her most famous "Fallaci," Oriana got Secretary of State Henry Kissinger to open up about some of his most intimate feelings about power. Until Fallaci's interview, Kissinger had revealed practically nothing about his life and personality. He had been described as a "loner," accused of being egocentric, but no reporter had been able to pierce through the cool demeanor of the man to learn what he felt about himself. Oriana Fallaci claims that her technique as an interviewer is simple. "I am not a thief of words at cocktail parties. I come into a room and set up my tape recorder and I take notes in my notebook. It is perfectly obvious what I am doing."

If you read carefully the transcripts of her interviews, it becomes clear that there is nothing simple or easy about her approach. She asks questions that force the subject to think about something he or she is used to answering glibly. One of her opening questions to Kissinger was "To what extent does power fascinate you? Try to be sincere."

Kissinger protested. He didn't think power fascinated him. He became defensive, telling Fallaci that the press had exaggerated his fascination with power.

Fallaci didn't let the matter rest. She immediately followed with another difficult question. "If your fascination with power was exaggerated, how do you explain your superstar status? Have you any theories?"

Kissinger answered, "Yes, but I won't tell you what they are."

Fallaci kept after him to admit his theory about why he had become such a diplomatic star.

"Well, why not," said Kissinger finally. "I'll tell you. Sometimes I see myself as a cowboy leading the caravan alone astride his horse, a wild west tale if you like."

That quote made headlines in papers around the world. Never before had Kissinger revealed such a romantic image of himself.

Why is it important that Kissinger reveal himself? Why do we have to know how he feels about himself. Isn't he entitled to privacy? Yet, Kissinger's actions affect our world. How he treats other world leaders is somewhat dependent on how he thinks of himself.

Knowing that Kissinger's image of himself as a man on horseback, alone, ahead of the crowd, is a valuable insight, both for readers today and future historians.

The ability to conduct newsworthy interviews has pushed Fallaci to the top of her field, one of the few women in such a position. She feels that being a woman is sometimes an advantage as a journalist, because she believes men in positions of power are occasionally more willing to let their guard down before a woman.

She started out in journalism by writing a crime column in an Italian daily paper. She won quick recognition and got to travel widely, covering revolutions and royal marriages, interviewing people all over the world.

In 1965, she became interested in the United States space program and the astronauts. She covered every aspect of the program, interviewing NASA engineers and workers, the astronauts, bureaucrats, even famed scientist Werner von Braun. The result was a lengthy book entitled *If the Sun Dies.*

The book opens in Los Angeles where Fallaci has gone to interview science fiction writer Ray Bradbury. Fallaci describes in great detail her personal reaction to Los Angeles. Nothing is moving except the cars; nothing grows but plastic. She takes a walk, and she feels she is the only one walking in Los Angeles. She trips and falls on the grass, only to discover that it has no smell, it really is plastic. There is no one to help her up, only cars, and cars don't have arms to reach out to her. She runs back to her motel room and tries to prick her finger on the cactus by the window sill, to prove to herself that something is really alive. The cactus is rubber. She goes to smell the rose in a vase on top of the TV, but it's glass and it shatters. "I had reached Los Angeles," she writes, "the first stage of my journey into the future and into myself."

Fallaci's musings about Los Angeles are not what one would expect in a book about the American space program. What does the description of a rubber cactus in a motel room have to do with the United States space program? Fallaci wants to let the reader know how she feels, not just what she saw. She believes that only if the reader journeys along with her feelings will the reader be able to understand. Her goal is to let the reader understand the way she had come to understand.

Fallaci is trying to do something more than just piece together, through papers and interviews, the workings of the United States space program. She is trying to use herself to answer the most important question: Why should anyone want to know about space astronauts and the moon?

She used the device of making the book a long letter to her father, a man who lives a comfortable life in the beautiful Chianti wine region of Italy. Fallaci's father believes the earth is good and beautiful, and that it is wasting money and effort to go to the moon because nothing grows there.

She frames the book as an extended debate with her father on whether or not the space program is worth learning about. She can't decide to give herself up wholeheartedly and with joy to plastic America, the root beer drive-ins, the clean, healthy nation of scientists and young space explorers; or to remain at home, in the fields populated with trees and birds, in the art and history of her native Florence.

As she interviews astronauts and scientists in Houston, Cape Kennedy, and Los Angeles, she tells the reader exactly how *she* is feeling all the time. There are many who feel that this type of personal journalism is an indulgence and ridiculous. When personal journalism is done well, however, it can involve the reader greatly and make him or her care. Personally, Fallaci's book on the space program interested me more than all the hundreds of other more conventional aritcles I have read about the astronauts.

A good example of her technique is Fallaci's interview with scientist Werner von Braun, developer of the rocket that sent the astronauts to the moon. Von Braun is a German scientist who came to America after World War II. In Germany, he had been responsible for the invention of the rockets which were used to bomb London. In seven months of bombing from Von Braun's "babies" as they were called, London suffered 3,000 dead and 68,000 wounded.

In January 1945, when it was obvious that Germany was losing the war, Von Braun called together his trusted co-workers and said, "Germany has lost the war, but our dream of going to the moon and to other planets isn't dead. The V-2's aren't only war weapons, they can be used for space travel. To one end or another, the Russians and Americans will want to know what we know. To which of them will it be better to leave our inheritance and dream?"

Everyone replied, "The Americans." Thus, it was that Von Braun and his colleagues wound up directing the United States space program. The space program has received much criticism and a lot of cutting jokes for being organized and dependent on a group of former Nazis. Von Braun was not a mere Nazi soldier, but a Nazi whose inventions had caused incredible death and destruction to both allies and to American troops in World War II.

Naturally, Fallaci who had lived through World War II, and whose earliest memories were of fighting against the Nazis and of Nazis arresting her father, was bound to have strong feelings about Von Braun.

She makes the reader feel the turmoil she was going through when she interviewed Von Braun. "He held out his huge hand, the hand of a strangler, and reached for mine. He had to stoop to reach it; I barely came up to his chest."

Fallaci writes that she was having trouble concentrating on the interview. She gives us a transcript of her interview and we can see that she is asking intelligent, detailed, and searching questions about the potential dangers of space exploration, about life on Mars. She is trying to find out why Von Braun has always wanted to send rockets out to explore space.

If only the transcript of the interview was read, it would be obvious that a competent reporter was con-

ducting a good interview. But Fallaci tells the reader
about the internal dialogue that was going on while
she was interviewing Von Braun. She kept smelling
lemon on Von Braun's breath, and the memory of the
lemon scent was disturbing. She can't remember
where she smelled that lemon scent before.

Von Braun concluded their interview with a moving statement on why he believes in space exploration.

> Men must always travel farther and farther afield. They
> must always widen their horizons and their interests;
> this is the will of God. If God didn't want it to be so,
> he wouldn't have given us the ability and the possi-
> bility to make progress and to change. If God didn't
> want it, he would stop us. Yes, of course, I'm reli-
> gious. Look I've known a lot of scientists and I've
> never known a scientist without some notion of God.
> Science tries to understand creation, but religion tries
> to understand the creator. It's a poor scientist who de-
> ludes himself that he can do without religion and God;
> the kind of scientist who scrapes the surface without
> looking beneath it. I try to look beneath the surface,
> and I see good there.

Usually, Dr. Von Braun is pictured as a "Dr.
Strangelove" character. In fact, the slightly mad, wheel-
chaired German scientist in the movie was supposedly
based on Von Braun, and it was rumored that Von
Braun was terribly hurt by the portrayal.

Fallaci shows that Von Braun is not the stereotype

of the cold, unfeeling ex-Nazi. She has allowed Von Braun to reveal himself as an ethical and religious man. "Odd," says Fallaci. "By all rights he should be unlikeable, and yet he isn't. For half an hour, I tried to make myself dislike him. To my utter astonishment, I found myself feeling just the opposite."

Fallaci has done a good job of reporting by simply showing the Von Braun that exists behind the stereotype. When Von Braun reveals his religious feelings, Fallaci has succeeded in exposing a new aspect of the man that most reporters missed, just as she was able to do with Kissinger in her interview with him.

Yet, Fallaci doesn't rest there. She can't be objective about this interview. By taking the reader into her confidence and telling us how greatly disturbed she was by the smell of lemon, Fallaci sets up a tension. There is something more to be revealed. Why does Fallaci find the smell of Von Braun disturbing? The reader wants to know.

Suddenly, Fallaci tells us. Toward the end of the interview with Von Braun, she is able to place where she has smelled that particular lemon scent before. It was the smell of the German soldiers coming to arrest her father and her father's friends.

As if in a daydream, Fallaci interrupts her reporting of the interview and talks to her father. "Remember," she says, "the German soldiers, all washed with disinfectant soap that smelled like lemon. We all loathed that scent of lemon."

Fallaci recalls for the reader her father's warning that you could always tell if somebody was a collaborator if he smelled of lemon. The boy who sat next to Fallaci in school used to smell of lemon, and he was always wanting to know where Oriana and her family hid when the Nazis came.

Then one day, the Nazis came to Oriana's house, smelling of lemon. Her father escaped that day, for a little while, but two Yugoslavian friends were captured, put on a train, and never came back.

At the conclusion of the interview, the reader feels what Fallaci has gone through interviewing Von Braun. She doesn't have to rely on a crude Nazi joke or reference to Dr. Strangelove.

Many might say that the "scent of lemon" has nothing to do with being a good journalist. But here, Fallaci has used that element to evoke in the reader a series of complex questions about the space program. Is there something sinister about an ex-Nazi in charge of the American trip to the moon? When a reporter makes us feel uncomfortable about something we would rather not think about, it is probably a strong indication that he or she is doing a good job.

3

Selwyn Raab:

The Confessions of George Whitmore

The newspapers pushed this boy into the electric chair, and the newspapers snatched him out of it. Blessed be the name of the newspapers.

—Defense lawyer for George Whitmore

Around noontime on a hot summer day, August 28, 1963, two young women just out of college and working in New York were brutally murdered in their Manhattan apartment. Someone entered the apartment of Janice Wylie and Emily Hoffert, knocked them unconscious, stabbed them numerous times, and tied them together with strips of sheets.

Their apartment was in a luxurious and seemingly safe building on Eighty-eighth Street, off Park Avenue in New York City. Despite the presence of a twenty-four-hour doorman and porters who manned the service elevator, the killer managed to enter and leave the building in the middle of a workday without being seen by either the doorman, the porter, or any of the other tenants. The bodies of the two girls were discovered by a third roommate who came home from work at the end of that day.

The story was an instant sensation because of the brutality of the act and because the girls were from the upper-middle class. Janice Wylie was the niece of a well-known author, Philip Wylie, and Emily Hoffert was the daughter of a prominent Minnesota physician. The case was instantly dubbed "The Career Girl Murders." Headlines ran daily in all New York papers. "AIR OF FEAR GRIPS SEDATE EAST SIDE" and "SLAIN GIRL'S FATHER: 'FORGETTING IS HARD' " were the titles of some of the lengthy articles on real or speculative aspects of the case. Television news programs filmed features on the story.

The twenty-third precinct of New York City's police department was responsible for finding the Wylie-Hoffert killer. Shortly after the murders were discovered, the apartment was thoroughly searched, fingerprints were taken, and all objects in the apartment studied. Within two days all residents and employees of the building had been questioned as well as the families of the girls, who gave the police the names of their daughters' employers, co-workers, and friends. Not one clue emerged. Fifty detectives were assigned to the case. They interviewed anyone who claimed to have known either of the girls or anyone who had any connection with the building they lived in. They followed up on hundreds of "leads" that were phoned into the police switchboard, usually by anonymous callers.

Additional detectives in the precinct house spent hours combing through police files looking for criminals whose M.O. (*modus operandi* or method of operation) seemed similar to that of the killer. A week after the murder, when still no clues had been discovered, experts from other city precincts were put on the case, bringing to one hundred the total number of men assigned to the Wylie-Hoffert case. It was the largest detail ever assigned to one crime in the history of New York. And still the case remained unsolved.

Eight months later, in the poor, black, and tenement area of Brownsville in Brooklyn, a minor crime occurred. Patrolman Frank C. Isola was on his beat shortly after one in the morning when he saw a man and woman go into an alley about eight feet from where he was standing. The man had his back to Isola, but Isola could see the man was holding the woman's pocketbook. The woman shrieked, and the man began to run. Isola yelled, "Stop, or I'll shoot," but the man had already ducked out of the alley through the side doorway of an adjacent building. Isola went after him. The man turned the corner of an intersection and disappeared.

The woman who screamed was a twenty-year-old nurse from Puerto Rico, Mrs. Ella Borrero, who lived in one of the buildings on the alley. Isola interviewed her and learned that she had been on her way home from work in a hospital downtown when a man appeared behind her and pulled her into the alley. The man grabbed her pocketbook and said he was going to rape her; at just that moment Isola had come into the alleyway. As the man started to flee, Mrs. Borrero yanked a button from his coat.

The precinct was a high-crime area, and a crime like this one was not unusual there. Patrolman Isola continued his normal shift and at 7 a.m. was making his final rounds. About two blocks from where the crime had occurred, Isola saw a young black man standing in the doorway of a launderette. He went up to the youth and asked what he was doing there; the boy said he was waiting for his brother to go to work with him. Isola asked to see his identification. Then the young man volunteered the information that he had been walking home from his girlfriend's house and had seen the chase of Mrs. Borrero's attacker.

He said the man had run up to him asking for help and then ran away again. Isola called up his sergeant who came to the launderette, and the two policemen had the boy repeat the entire story. They took it down in their notebooks, including the witness's name as "George Whitman."

Isola returned to the precinct and told his supervising detective about the boy's account. Although the detective was not interested himself and sent Isola home, he passed the information on to another detective, Richard Aidala, who was very interested.

Aidala had been investigating the murder of a woman named Minnie Edmonds, which had occurred nine days earlier in an alley one block from this latest incident. Aidala had not found the Edmonds' murderer and looked upon this boy's account as a possible link. His co-worker, Detective Joseph DiPrima thought so, too, and they decided to pick up the boy for questioning.

On April 24, at 7 a.m., Aidala and Isola visited the launderette and saw the boy who they stopped and asked for identification. The youth produced his driver's license which identified him as George Whitmore, Jr., a resident of Wildwood, New Jersey. The two policemen decided to take him to the precinct.

As they began to question Whitmore, Mrs. Borrero was brought to the station also and placed outside the door of the room. She was too short to see through the peephole, so she balanced on a stool. She looked at Whitmore and said, "This is the man." To be certain, she asked that she be able to hear his voice. Isola went in the room and had Whitmore say, "I'm going to rape you." Mrs. Borrero listened and then repeated, "This is the man. This is the man." Within minutes, Aidala placed George Whitmore under arrest for attempted rape.

By 4:12 a.m. on Saturday, after almost nine hours of interrogation, the deputy police commissioner of New York, Walter Arm, was awakened by a telephone call from Manhattan Chief of Detectives McKearney who had surprising news to report: In a Brooklyn station house a young man named George Whitmore had confessed to the attempted rape of Mrs. Ella Borrero, the murder of Mrs. Minnie Edmonds, and, most astonishing of all, the murders of Janice Wylie and Emily Hoffert.

Whitmore was driven to criminal court in Brooklyn, where, because he was poor, a lawyer was appointed to represent him at his plea hearing. By this time every newspaper in the city carried the news that the career-girl murders had been solved, and the murderer was George Whitmore, Jr. Due to the seriousness of the charges, the judge ordered Whitmore jailed without bail until the actual indictments (the formal charging with a crime by the grand jury) took place. Whitmore's appointed lawyer, Jerome J. Leftow met with him over the weekend at the House of Detention for Youth in Brooklyn, and was stunned by their first conversation:

Leftow: Listen, anything you say to me is confidential. I'm here to make sure your rights are protected. Are any of these charges true?

Whitmore: No, I didn't do these things.

Leftow: The police say you admitted these crimes. Is that true?

Whitmore: Yes, I admitted them, but it's not true that I did these things.

Leftow: Than why did you admit them?

Whitmore: They beat me and scared me into confessing. I didn't know what they wanted from me. I didn't know I was charged with murder until I saw you in court.

Leftow: Have you spoken to anyone else about what happened to you?

Whitmore: No, I didn't have the chance to speak to anybody. Except for the cops, you're the first person I spoke to since my arrest.

Whitmore then told Leftow the details of his interrogation. Their conversation lasted for over two hours.

By Friday, May 8, George Whitmore was indicted for all three crimes. His lawyer entered pleas of "not guilty" for each charge. Then, by order of State Supreme Court Justice Charles Marks, Whitmore was ordered to Bellevue Hospital where he was to be given a complete psychiatric examination.

Sometime during the summer, while George Whitmore was still in the prison ward of Bellevue, a twenty-nine-year-old reporter for *The World Telegram and Sun* was digging through his paper's files for some background material on a series of articles he was writing. Selwyn Raab's subject was police brutality.

"I had been doing a variety of stories and one story that had come to my attention was a story that involved the shooting of a young Puerto Rican kid. It was a mistaken identity case, where some kid had been mistakenly identified by an off-duty cop who was drunk and he shot the kid and almost killed him.

"While I was working on this—it was the following summer after the Wylie-Hoffert murder—I had been routinely going through the clips on police brutality, I noticed there was a line in one of the stories about Whitmore; that he had charged police brutality on the day he was arraigned.

"I hadn't worked on any of it, and I hadn't kept in touch with it at all. But what was peculiar was that I had worked on a lot of stories about mental health laws in New York and the rights of mental patients. And Whitmore had been sent to Bellevue—and he had been there for over three months!"

What bothered Raab was that he knew from his own research on the subject that court-ordered psychiatric examinations on individuals rarely exceeded thirty days.

"They usually get a report in a month. There's not supposed to be a long delay, because that's just a holding operation. So that piqued my curiosity.

"I started making some phone calls. I thought there might just be a good story in it. Not acquitting him, you know, but either that they found him so insane or that there was something so peculiar about him that they had to do all these tests.

"Anyway there was something smelly there—something peculiar. And what I got on my phone calls was —I got the old curtain of silence—from everybody."

Raab was confused by the fact that it had not yet been announced which of the three charges Whitmore would be brought up on first. Whitmore was under the jurisdiction of both the Brooklyn and Manhattan District Attorneys' Offices, and though the Wylie-

Hoffert crime was the most serious of the charges, as well as the one that occurred first, Manhattan D.A. Frank Hogan refused to announce a trial date. To Raab, that seemed fishy: "Presumably, they were going to bring him up on the murder case; it was the only thing which would make sense. You don't try a guy for spitting on the sidewalk at the same time he's held on a serious charge."

Deciding to dig further, Raab contacted Whitmore's lawyer, Jerome Leftow, but got nowhere. Leftow felt it would be unethical to discuss the case out of court and declined to meet with any reporters. It was impossible for Raab to see Whitmore himself. At that time, in the mid-1960s, reporters were not allowed to visit anyone held in custody; nor were they allowed to correspond with prisoners. Today, in some states reporters are allowed to talk to prisoners, but at the time Raab had no way of getting to Whitmore.

And that left only one source of investigation, George's mother and sisters. Raab met with Mrs. Whitmore and right away was stunned: her son, she claimed, was nowhere near Manhattan on the day of the Wylie-Hoffert murder. He had spent the day—in fact, the entire summer—in Wildwood, New Jersey. Figuring that Wildwood was a two-hour drive from New York, and therefore still a possible back-and-forth trip, Raab went down to Wildwood to see if anyone there remembered seeing George around noontime on that day.

It took several trips to the seashore town, but Raab was fortunate. Although a year had passed since August 23, 1963, most people in George's neighborhood remembered exactly where they had been on that day. It was the day of the March on Washington, and most Black-Americans in Wildwood, as well as throughout the country, had spent the day in front of their television sets watching Martin Luther King at the historic occasion. Several of them recalled that George Whitmore had been watching television in the lobby of the Ivey Hotel, with a girl named Luci Montgomery.

On Raab's first visit to Wildwood, he discovered another confusing piece of information. When the police had booked Whitmore, they gave as their reason for questioning him on the Wylie-Hoffert murders the fact that they had found in his possession a particular snapshot. That photo was of a white girl sitting on the hood of a car. One of the policemen in the Brooklyn interrogation room at that time had been helping out on the Manhattan murder case, and he claimed the girl in the picture looked exactly like Janice Wylie. So they then began grilling Whitmore on the Wylie-Hoffert case. Whitmore said he had picked up the snapshot in a garbage dump, and he had no idea who the girl was, but he had kept the picture so that his friends would think he had a pretty white girlfriend, a mark of status in their eyes. The police had not believed him. Then, under pressure, Whitmore began to break down and confess that the girl was who the police were telling him it was, and that he had murdered her.

Raab took a copy of the photograph around Wildwood, and, sure enough, somebody remembered the girl in the picture as a former resident of Wildwood, now married and living somewhere else. Raab located Mrs. Arlene Franco in Philadelphia, and she verified that it was her picture, and that she had given it to a girlfriend. Raab found the friend, who corroborated Mrs. Franco's identification and added that she herself had discarded the photo when she was about to move from Wildwood.

Raab was astonished. How could the police try George Whitmore for the Wylie-Hoffert murders when their one connecting link between him and the victims turned out to be no connection at all. What was even *more* astonishing was that Arlene Franco told Raab that detectives from Manhattan District Attorney Hogan's office also had been down to see her and she had *told them* that it was her picture. If that was true, thought Raab,—and there was no reason to doubt Mrs. Franco—then the D.A. had known Whitmore wasn't the right man. Still there had been no hint by the police that they had made a mistake.

Raab returned to New York where he learned to his shock that Whitmore was to be tried on the charge of attempting to rape Mrs. Ella Borrero. The headlines of the city papers were still playing up Whitmore's confession to the horrible "career girl murders." It was going to be hard for the defense to find jurors who had not been influenced by the press. Raab expected any day to see the police announce that Whitmore was not guilty of the more serious crime, but they remained silent.

Meanwhile, Raab tried to get to Whitmore's lawyer to make sure that Leftow had learned of the evidence of Whitmore's innocence that Raab had unearthed. The lawyer refused to talk to Raab saying, "Don't worry, I don't want any interference from you guys." Raab held off writing his stories on the Whitmore evidence, thinking that Leftow perhaps had a strategy Raab didn't understand. "I held off because I wanted to see what would happen. I thought he [Leftow] was going to spring a surprise in that case, maybe call for a mistrial on the basis of other evidence. I even thought he would oppose that attempted rape trial on the basis that there were two other murder charges that should be straightened out first. Again the assumption was that he knew what he was doing. But then I watched

the trial and it was obvious he didn't know what he
was doing. It was the first case he ever tried in court
and he was really out of it, out of his depth."

On November 18, Whitmore was convicted of attempted rape and assault. Raab felt frustrated. He had
given Whitmore's lawyers the benefit of the doubt, and
still Whitmore wasn't free. The lawyers had not used
the evidence Raab had found. Raab felt it was time
to start writing why he believed Whitmore innocent.
Raab had located Luci Montgomery, the girl who had
watched television with George in New Jersey at the
exact time the murders were committed.

Yet, because Whitmore had previously confessed to
the crime, not even Raab's editors had much faith in
the new evidence. Instead of placing Raab's story on
page one, it appeared on the back pages of *The World
Telegram*. Raab had his own explanation of why he
was ignored.

"Everyone was so convinced. This was the biggest,
most brutal murder case. And no one wanted to take
a chance. No one could believe that the cops would
make such a horrendous mistake. Especially D.A.
Hogan's office. Everyone would say, 'Well, you know,
they might make mistakes elsewhere, but not there.'
Then there was the confession. Everyone would come
back at me and say, 'What about the confession? How
do you account for that?' People at that time couldn't

readily accept that the police might use tactics—might get a confession that way."

"I was even willing to give away the scoop," says Raab, "because I was so frustrated over the lack of coverage we [his own paper] were giving the story." Even though Raab did try to pass his story on to reporters from other papers, no paper was willing to run a story stating that Whitmore was probably innocent and that his confession had been taken by force.

Raab received a telephone call from Mrs. Whitmore, who asked his help in finding another lawyer. Raab first tried the Legal Defense Fund of the NAACP, but they didn't see any reason to interfere because Whitmore had confessed; his civil rights hadn't been violated. Raab pleaded for help. "Whitmore's civil rights *had* been violated," said Raab. "Someone was withholding evidence. The police had the wrong man." But still no offers of help were forthcoming.

Finally, Stanley Reiben, a Brooklyn trial lawyer with a long record of winning cases, agreed to represent Whitmore. Immediately Reiben moved for a mistrial on the rape verdict, citing information that at least one of the jurors had come to the trial with strong antiblack feelings and the belief that Whitmore was guilty of the Wylie-Hoffert murders. And Reiben was quick to make use of Raab's evidence.

Then on January 26, 1965, District Attorney Ho-

gan's office announced the arrest of Richard Robles
for the murders of Janice Wylie and Emily Hoffert.

Who was Richard Robles and how had he been
found? Why was he suspected of the crime? And for
how long had Manhattan police known about him?
It soon became known that the police had suspected
Robles from the first, right after a dope-peddling
friend of his had accused him of the crime. Raab was
incensed that the D.A. had allowed Whitmore to stand
trial with the murder suspicion hanging over him
while all the time the police and the D.A. suspected
that someone else had committed the Wylie-Hoffert
crime.

Today, with hindsight, Raab can talk calmly about
what at the time he considered a grave and infuriating
injustice. "My own feeling of conjecture is that they
didn't want to acquit Whitmore until they had somebody else . . . because of the disgrace involved. Hogan
later said that the reason he was so reluctant to say
anything about Whitmore was that they were on the
trail of Robles, but didn't want him to know, which
was absurd because Robles *did* know. They had questioned him the first week after the murder; he had
found police microphones hidden in his apartment. It
was absurd . . . totally absurd. And that to me was
the major disgrace in the case—allowing Whitmore
to go on trial for that attempted rape knowing that
they had a stinking, rotten case."

In the last week of April, George Whitmore, now cleared of suspicion in the Wylie-Hoffert case, stood trial for the murder of Minnie Edmonds, the second of his alleged confessions. By now press interest in Whitmore was great, this time on his behalf. Raab and Whitmore's attorney did everything possible to encourage the belief that if one confession had been false, there was reason to believe the others were untrue. The police had no hard evidence against Whitmore. The jury came back undecided. There would have to be another trial.

Meanwhile, Whitmore remained in jail. His conviction for the attempted rape of Mrs. Borrero was overturned, and he had to stand trial on the charge again. Raab concentrated his efforts on trying to clear Whitmore of the Borrero rape charges.

At the second Borrero trial, there was an all white jury, plus Mrs. Borrero's evidence that Whitmore was the man who attacked her. Patrolman Isola and Detectives Aidala and DiPrima testified that Whitmore had confessed voluntarily to the crime. The judge would not allow Whitmore's attorney to make any reference to the Wylie-Hoffert confession, particularly to support the argument that the Borrero confession was invalid. Finally, the prosecutor had a button that Mrs. Borrero had pulled from her assailant's coat. The prosecutor made much of the fact that Whitmore's coat had buttons missing from it.

On March 25, 1966, nearly two years after he was first arrested, Whitemore was found guilty of attempted rape.

Raab was disappointed, but as convinced as ever of Whitmore's innocence. For the next six years, Raab was to devote a major part of his time and work toward proving Whitmore's innocence. During that time Raab's newspaper closed down and Raab began working for Channel 13, the public television station in New York City. For six years Whitmore remained in jail but Raab still believed Whitmore was innocent.

Raab had discovered several holes in the case against Whitmore for the rape of Mrs. Borrero, but none were enough to convince a jury. Whitmore's girlfriend and her mother testified that Whitmore had been in their apartment at the time the attack on Mrs. Borrero was taking place. They were, however, confused on the exact times, and the jury did not accept their testimony. Raab believed them, though, and he had another lead to track down now: He had heard a rumor, from another reporter, that the "button connection" in the Borrero case was a phony.

Acting on a hunch that the D.A. might have sent the button to the FBI Crime Lab for tests, Raab contacted a friend who had good connections with the bureau. "And I said, 'Will you check and see if there's a report on the button?' And I got a copy of the report, which I took over to the Whitmore defense. And the report said that the strands from the button and the strands from Whitmore's coat were completely different."

Raab also saw enormous discrepancies between Mrs. Borrero's identification of George in the precinct and the description she had originally given Patrolman Isola, the one that had come out over the teletype alarm. The teletype description was for an older, heavier man, and made no mention of other distinguishing characteristics. The fact was, however, that George Whitmore suffered from a very bad case of acne; his face was covered with pimples and running sores, and anyone in his presence would have noticed it. Yet the teletype description had not mentioned his complexion. And Patrolman Isola, who ran across Whitmore later that night never really made the connection between the description and the boy in front of him. Raab says, "Isola comes across him five hours later and hasn't got the *slightest* suspicions. The police tried to explain that away by saying that he was an inexperienced officer. Humbug! That was all he was concerned about that night! He was working overtime, he was so interested in the case, and here's a guy . . . the one cop who chases the guy and he's not interested in Whitmore. Obviously, Whitmore didn't fit the description."

Furthermore, Raab saw no way that Whitmore could have covered the distance from his girlfriend's apartment to Mrs. Borrero's building in the time allowed. He even tried *running* the distance and couldn't do it.

But the real break in the Borrero case occurred in the summer of 1972. Raab describes the events leading up to it:

"What happened was they had lost all their appeals in the state courts. George had been out on bail pending the appeal. And then they threw the book at him and sentenced him to five to ten years. The Court of Appeals voted 4 to 3 against a new trial, and so George had his bail revoked and had to go back to jail.

"I'd spoken to Arthur Beldock; he was the latest lawyer. I'd told him everything that I knew and Beldock frankly seemed first-rate . . . hallelujah! It was a hopeless case, but at least there was somebody who had some savvy. Really a classy lawyer. His father had been the Chief of the Appellate Division in Brooklyn—a well-known family.

"So, anyway, he made a motion in federal court in Brooklyn. I went there. George was now in custody. In fact, the State had him. Beldock went in to argue . . . and it was a beautiful courtroom . . . with nobody there, and I remembered all those days when Reiben had lawyers and people all over. But this time it was George Beldock, a state prosecutor, somebody representing the State Attorney General's Office and also the Brooklyn D.A.'s Office. And myself and Mrs. Whitmore, and one of his sisters, his sister Geraldine . . . in a big court . . . it was empty.

"The judge denied bail, refused to do anything, so George had to serve his sentence . . . he was going to Greenhaven.

"We had a very somber drive back, Beldock and myself. And somehow or other we sort of looked at each other and I said, 'You know, I'm not going to let it happen. I know this guy is innocent. And he's never gotten his day in court. It's eight years later, but let them hear the full evidence.' And Beldock said simply, 'We'll have one more meeting to try to figure out what to do.' "

Raab and Beldock met, and went over the evidence again. They also went back and checked all their previous leads; some had paid off while others had fizzled out. One apparent lead that had seemed to go nowhere was an entry in Patrolman Isola's notebook made on the night of the Borrero attack. It said, "sister-in-law, Mrs. Viroet [with a phone number] said she saw man in the street," followed by a description of the man. It was a description far different from George Whitmore's.

Beldock had a private investigator working for him named Richard Tracy, and the three men decided the only thing left to do was to see if Mrs. Viroet existed and could be located.

Raab recalls that he said, " 'Look, let's try the phone book route. Let's look for every Viroet in the New York phone book. I'm also going to try the telephone company. Try to retrace that number.' We knew the number was disconnected by now, but if we could find that old number, that '63 number, maybe, she was still around New York.

"Tried it. And it didn't work. So we divvied up the phone books. I took Manhattan and Brooklyn, and the private investigator started with Queens and the Bronx. And he hit somebody! A Viroet in the Bronx who said he remembered somebody living in that neighborhood who had moved to Puerto Rico in 1965 or 1966. And they had run a grocery store and we knew that Mrs. Viroet had run a grocery store—a bodega.

"He was not a relative and we knew it was a long shot. All he knew was that these Viroets had moved to Puerto Rico, and that they had a bar, and he thought the name was 'Orange.' And the detective got the story back to us—the detective was really funny—and came back and said all he knew was 'Green Island.' That was what he came back with.

"And then the detective died during the summer, a natural death. And Beldock and I were meeting periodically. So we knew 'Green Island,' 'Viroet,' and 'Orange.' A bar with 'Orange' in its name. What do you do with that?!"

Raab right away figured out that "Green Island" translated into Spanish was Isla Verde, a section of San Juan near the airport. They went through the entire San Juan phone book looking for anything with the word "orange" in it. There was nothing; and no "Viroet" either. Raab felt someone had to nose around Isla Verde in person. But his employer, Channel 13, would not agree to send him down there on what seemed to be such a tenuous clue. He would have to rely on somebody already down there.

Working at Channel 13, on Raab's news program, was a girl named Maria Mena, whose uncle lived in Puerto Rico. Raab had Maria ask her uncle if he would drive around Isla Verde and look for a bar with something like "orange" in its name. It took him two months to get back to them.

"And sometime in October or November, he called back and he said, 'There *is* a bar, not far from the Racquet Club; it's called 'El Narangal' which means 'The Orange Grove.' I said, 'Please don't do anything. Just go in there, in the bar, and find out if there's a "Viroet" there. Don't say anything else.' And he called

back about two weeks later and said, 'Yes, there *is* a
Viroet there. They told me they had moved over from
Brooklyn.' "

With the odds somewhat improved, Raab and Beldock flew to San Juan, taking along Maria Mena as
their interpreter. Though they were certain they now
had the right Mrs. Viroet, they did not know whether
she would talk to them and if she did, whether she
could offer any help to George's case.

"We had all this information but we didn't know
what would happen at all. So, we went down there
and arrived on a Thursday night, and Friday morning
we drove over to the bar—it was a sort of half-bar,
half-cafe-type place. Maria went in and talked to Mrs.
Viroet—it was the right Mrs. Viroet. She was reluctant
to talk but she had all this information. It was amaz-
ing. So we said we'd come back that evening. We
came back and she told us the entire story."

Mrs. Viroet said that she had seen her sister-in-law,
Mrs. Borrero, walking across the street that night with
a man, that after the incident Mrs. Borrero had given
her a description of a man completely different from
George Whitmore. Furthermore, Mrs. Viroet said the
day after the attack, Mrs. Borrero had gone down to
the station and had identified someone other than
Whitmore as her assailant. Mrs. Viroet had told all
this to the police when they questioned her, but as it
did not support Mrs. Borrero's story, the police simply

chose to overlook it. Mrs. Viroet agreed to sign an affidavit for Raab and Beldock.

"So we were up that whole evening writing out the affidavit and translating Spanish into English, one back to the other. She was very nice. But she would not allow us to film her. She would not be on television.

"But she signed it. It was evidence that pointed out all the inconsistencies in Mrs. Borrero's evidence. And that was that."

Raab, armed with the affidavit, returned to New York and called on Brooklyn's new district attorney, Eugene Gold. He showed Gold the affidavit and told him that he, Raab, was going to run a story on the case on his program, "The 51st State." Raab suggested that Gold might want to have the charges dropped against George Whitmore.

One month later, the charges were dropped and Whitmore was released from jail. It had taken nine years, but finally there was no doubt as to Whitmore's innocence. The confessions had not been valid.

The intervening years had also seen drastic new developments in America's system of justice and particularly in those procedures governing the rights of the accused. Spurred by the press and public outrage that an innocent man could conceivably wind up in the electric chair, the New York State Legislature forbade capital punishment.

Laws were also enacted allowing those confined for crimes to have access to the press and to be able to exchange correspondence with individual reporters. And, most important, on June 13, 1966, the U.S. Supreme Court ruled in the case of *Miranda v. Arizona* that no suspect—juvenile or adult—could be interrogated by police without first having been advised of his right to have a lawyer present. The *Miranda* decision was not made retroactive, and thus did not help George Whitmore obtain his freedom. But his case had been cited in the ruling as evidence of the need for new interrogation procedures, and the court could not help but be aware of the miscarriage of justice that had been forced on George Whitmore.

Selwyn Raab did run the Whitmore case on his "51st State" program. And it is one of the stories of which he is most proud. In 1973, he was awarded a citation by the New York Press Club for his television coverage of the Whitmore story.

Selwyn Raab became involved with the Whitmore case almost a year after George Whitmore's arrest, and only because it related to other work he was doing at the time. But his instincts for truth, his immediate sensation that there was something wrong made him stick with the story until he was sure of its resolution. Raab described his perseverance this way:

"I wasn't out to show up the police or 'the system.'

You just feel that somebody ought to be looking into things . . . . I spent sleepless nights knowing Whitmore was in jail and knowing he was innocent . . . and there was the frustration, the need to unravel the truth."

Raab is an investigative reporter who trusts his own instincts for truth but also recognizes that those instincts must be borne out in the facts of a story.

I asked him if he had ever wanted to be anything other than a reporter, a lawyer perhaps. His reply was instantaneous: "Never. The law, a trial, has no logic in it. There's no truth, contrary to what people think. There's no logic to what comes out in a courtroom. There's no guarantee that truth will come out. I'd never want to be a lawyer."

"But while you were watching all the Whitmore trials," I asked, "and feeling as strongly as you did that the lawyers were mishandling the case, didn't you ever wish you could just storm onto the floor and take over the case?"

"No," said Selwyn Raab. "I just wanted *them* to be better lawyers. But I didn't want to do it myself. I did what was my job. I wanted them to do *their* jobs."

In 1974, Raab won the 1974 Heywood Broun Award from the Newspaper Guild for his articles revealing once again new evidence that called into question the murder convictions of a man, this time Rubin (Hurricane) Carter, a boxer.

4

Edward R. Murrow:

Choosing Sides

Ideally, in the case of controversial issues the audience should be left with no impression as to which side the analyst himself actually favors.

—Paul White, former head of CBS News

When the medium that an investigating journalist chooses is television, there is an almost automatic impact of importance that is created when the camera focuses on *any* person or event. Therefore, the choice of subject for a television report is an especially sensitive one.

Edward R. Murrow, probably the most esteemed American television reporter, understood the power of television. He knew each time he chose a subject to be studied on his weekly CBS "See It Now" program, the odds were great that the particular subject would become important to millions of Americans. In 1953 and 1954 Edward R. Murrow chose to expose McCarthyism.

In the early fifties, the United States was caught up in a wave of hysteria and fear over the influence of communism on the "American Way of Life." Republican Senator Joseph R. McCarthy of Wisconsin was chairman of the Senate Subcommittee on Investigations, which he used to find supposed communists in the government. McCarthy would stand before the television cameras, waving sheets of papers and shout, "I have the names of 205 card-carrying communists in the State Department!" Nobody ever got to see the papers he was waving or a full list of the names, but many people believed McCarthy's charges and shared his fear of communist subversion.

The senator used the power of his committee to go after supposed communists even if he had only the flimsiest evidence to support his charges. McCarthy believed that a person should not hold a job in the government if there were merely suspicion or rumors that he was a communist. The true viciousness of his thinking meant that if someone didn't like you, they could start a rumor that you were a communist and you could lose your job. McCarthy argued that the threat of communist subversion was so great that communists had to be rooted out by any means. McCarthyism ruined the lives and careers of many individuals. Hundreds of corporations and businesses decided that the only safe course of action was to make sure that all "leftist" individuals were fired. "Black" lists were drawn up of people who might be considered sympathetic to the ideals or goals of the Soviet Union, people who had relatives or friends who might be leftists, or even those who had once made remarks critical of United States policies. If your name got on a blacklist, there was no way of fighting it. No trials were held. No proof was needed. It meant you could not work in your profession any longer.

Edward R. Murrow knew people whose lives had been ruined by the blacklists of McCarthyism. One of his friends had committed suicide. Murrow believed that his friend's tragedy was an inevitable consequence of the kind of tactics used by McCarthy and his supporters. Murrow wanted to do something to stem the tide of hysteria before more lives were ruined. Murrow's friend committed suicide in 1948, but Murrow did not attempt an exposé on McCarthyism until five years later. Nothing shows more clearly how strong the grip of fear was on all newsmen than the fact that Murrow felt it necessary to remain silent for five years.

For in 1948, Murrow was already one of the most widely respected journalists in the land. Today only

Walter Cronkite approximates the kind of respect and emotional attachment most Americans associate with Murrow. During World War II, news about conditions in Europe came to the United States via the strong clear voice of Edward R. Murrow. Murrow described the scene from the rooftops during the German bombing of London, and millions of Americans shared his horror at the Nazi bombings, and his love for the gallantry of the British. In time, Murrow came to symbolize that gallantry under fire.

After the war, Murrow's popularity, his distinctive low voice, and his lean and appealing physical presence made his transition from a radio personality to a television personality an easy one. By the early 1950s he had two programs of his own on CBS, "Person to Person" and "See It Now," as well as a nightly fifteen-minute news and commentary broadcast. Murrow was clearly the most trusted man in television. But for five long years, he waited, afraid to take the enormous risks involved in trying to expose McCarthyism for the unfair witch hunt that it was.

One day in October, 1953, Murrow was scheduled to have lunch with the executive producer of "See It Now," Fred Friendly. Murrow appeared late and handed his colleague a crumpled up piece of paper as a way of explanation. It was a newspaper clipping. Friendly and Murrow had both been on the lookout for a way to expose the tactics of McCarthyism. Murrow handed Friendly the clipping saying, "It may be our case history. It's the story of an Air Force lieutenant who is losing his commission because his father and his sister are supposed to be left-wing sympathizers. Let's have someone check it out."

A CBS reporter was sent to Dexter, Michigan, where Air Force Lieutenant Milo J. Radulovich lived. Radulovich was a twenty-six-year-old meteorologist in the Air Force Reserve, who was being asked to resign because his father and sister were supposedly radicals. Radulovich refused to resign quietly. An Air Force Board of Inquiry ordered him removed from the service on the grounds that he was a security risk, but the board never specified what the exact charges against Radulovich were. They would not tell Radulovich who was accusing him of being a security risk, or what proof they had. The board said it had no doubt as to Radulovich's loyalty to the United States, but he was a security risk because of the alleged beliefs of his relatives.

The Radulovich case was a striking example of guilt by association—the firing of a young man for nonspecified views "allegedly held" by members of his family. The film crew sent their story back to New York. The film included conversations with Radulovich's father, a World War I veteran who had left Poland to live in the United States forty years before;

a clip of the lieutenant's sister refusing to discuss her political beliefs and arguing that those beliefs, whatever they were, had nothing to do with her brother; a stirring defense of Radulovich by the head of the American Legion in Dexter; as well as other residents of the town who knew and supported the entire Radulovich family. The "See It Now" crew had assembled in its interviews some very convincing evidence on the dangers of McCarthyism. But the most convincing evidence of all was provided by the words of Milo Radulovich himself:

> If I am being judged by my relatives . . . are my children going to be asked to denounce me? Are they going to be asked what their father was labeled? Are they going to have to explain to their friends why their father's a security risk? . . . This is a chain reaction if the thing is let stand . . . I see a chain reaction that has no end.

Watching the film Murrow knew the Radulovich story was the perfect piece he had been searching for, a small but dramatic picture of injustices resulting from the anticommunist hysterics of that day. The lieutenant's case could show viewers across the country that the tactics of McCarthy posed a real threat to every person living in America. If the young, loyal, and conscientious Radulovich in Dexter, Michigan, could lose his job and have his reputation ruined, it could happen to anyone.

Murrow knew this broadcast would be the most controversial of his career. During the frantic weekend of editing over five hours of film into a half-hour program, Murrow told Friendly to allow him about four minutes at the end of the program for his commentary. "Leave me enough time," he said, "because we are going to live or die by our ending. Management is going to howl, and we may blow ourselves right out of the water, but we simply can't do an 'on the other hand' ending for this."

Even today, most television documentaries conclude with that "try to present the other side of an issue" ending. Twenty years later, the "See It Now" show on Milo Radulovich still has a strong impact because we are not used to television reporters taking a stand. "We believe," said Murrow at the end of the program, "that the son shall not bear the iniquity of the father, even though that iniquity be proved beyond all doubt, which in this case it was not. . . . Whatever happens in this whole area of the relationship between the individual and the state, we will do ourselves; it cannot be blamed upon Malenkov, Mao Tse-tung or even our allies. It seems to us—that is, to Fred Friendly and myself—that it is a subject that should be argued about endlessly."

The show ended. The camera and the lights went off. Within sixty seconds, everyone in the studio was pushing his way toward Murrow to offer congratulations. CBS switchboards lit up across the control room; correspondents from all over the country called to tell how much they appreciated the show. The CBS switchboard was jammed and after one thousand calls, the operators stopped counting. Most were favorable, including an important one from the advertising manager of Alcoa, who expressed his company's pride in having sponsored the program. The next's day mail was overwhelming. Some viewers complained that Murrow and CBS had "sided" with the enemies of the United States in doing the documentary; most had only words of praise for the courage in tackling the subject of guilt by association. It seemed as if finally somebody had stood up and said what a lot of people had wanted to hear and say for a long time but were afraid to do.

The story of Milo Radulovich represented a departure from the usual standards of television journalism. Murrow had offered the Air Force a chance to present its case, but he had said quite strongly that there were no two sides to this issue. Murrow was convinced that the "See It Now" staff had assembled enough facts to prove that a severe injustice had been committed, and he was unwilling to pretend that an argument could be made for defending the firing of Radulovich.

One month later Murrow had the pleasure of an-

nouncing on the air that the Air Force was reversing
its decision. Secretary of the Air Force Harold E.
Talbott announced on the air that, "It is consistent
with the interests of the national security to retain
Lieutenant Radulovich in the United States Air Force.
He is not, in my opinion, a security risk."

Having won once, Murrow realized television was
capable of doing much more. Only television, he felt,
could educate and alert the American public to the
dangers of McCarthyism. For years, Murrow had been
criticized by a few of his friends and colleagues for
not tackling McCarthyism straight on. Murrow had
felt it would have been useless to merely attack Mc-
Carthy with words, to wind up trading charges with
McCarthy. He felt he had to show people, through the
television camera, what McCarthyism was, what it
could do to people and to the country. Murrow believed that the camera could attack more accurately
and with more devastating effect than his words.

For years, Murrow had in the back of his mind the
idea of doing a "See It Now" program on the senator
himself. A camera crew had been collecting footage
on McCarthy. The film piled up, but Murrow had not
made any move to use it. After the Radulovich broadcast, however, he began looking through what they
had accumulated on McCarthy. By the beginning of
1954, the project was on: "See It Now" began to prepare

a March 9 program on the subject of Joseph Mc-
Carthy.

The McCarthy program was considered so important that practically every writer, reporter, and tech-
nician was pulled off other projects to concentrate
exclusively on this one. Murrow's biggest fear was
that "See It Now" simply would not have enough material on the senator to justify a strong show.

The format for the broadcast was simple. It was to
consist of the collected film of Senator McCarthy with
a running commentary by Murrow throughout the
film. There were scenes from several of the senator's
more explosive committee sessions and speeches: Mc-
Carthy attacking World War II hero General Ralph
Zwicker for allowing a dentist who had taken the fifth
amendment to remain in the army; McCarthy grilling
State Department official Reed Harris about a book he
wrote while in college in which he attacked football,
McCarthy implying that anyone who attacked football
should not be allowed in the State Department.

Each film was chosen to show one of McCarthy's
methods, and after each clip, Murrow intervened to
point out the inaccuracies, innuendos, and deceptions
being used by the senator. Throughout the film, the
camera panned close on McCarthy's face, his nervous
twitches, his sneers and grimaces. The message came
across clearly. In addition to his tactics, and apart

from any other considerations, McCarthy was a very
unattractive person. The total effect was devastating—
so much so that many staff members grew very nervous about the impending broadcast. Anyone watching
the show would realize this was not a balanced report.
It was a half hour designed to show McCarthy in the
worst light possible.

Several days before the show, the entire staff was
convened to discuss the program. Each member was
asked his opinion about the substance and format and
if there was anything in his or her background that
Joe McCarthy might later be able to use as a weapon
against CBS or a smear against "See It Now." Luckily,
there were no vulnerable spots.

On Tuesday, March 9, 1954, at 10:30 p.m., the
McCarthy broadcast began with Murrow reading from
his script. "The line between investigating and perse-
cuting is a very fine one, and the junior senator from
Wisconsin has stepped over it repeatedly." When the
film was over, Murrow concluded the broadcast.

> We will not be driven by fear into an age of unrea-
> son, if we dig deep into our own history and our doc-
> trine and remember that we are not descended from
> fearful men, not from men who feared to write, to
> speak, to associate, and to defend causes which were
> for the moment unpopular.
>
> This is no time for men who oppose Senator Mc-
> Carthy's methods to keep silent. We can deny our
> heritage and our history, but we cannot escape respon-

sibility for the result. There is no way for a citizen of
a republic to abdicate his responsibilities. . . .

Cassius was right. The fault, dear Brutus, is not in
our stars but in ourselves. Good night and good luck.

The public's response was overwhelmingly in favor
of the program (within one day CBS reported it had
received the largest response ever generated by any of
its programs. The 12,348 remarks ran 15 to 1 in
Murrow's favor). Within a very short time of that
broadcast, Joseph McCarthy's career was finished. His
fellow senators censured him. McCarthy decided not
to run for the Senate again. He died a year later.

Many argued that the "See It Now" broadcast
brought about McCarthy's fall from popularity. After
the broadcast, a floodgate of criticism of McCarthy and
McCarthyism was opened. Senators, army officials,
cabinet members, and other public figures who had
previously remained silent now felt obligated to speak
out.

Murrow refused to take the credit for ending Mc-
Carthyism, perhaps because he realized that he had
manipulated television just as McCarthy had. Mc-
Carthy used television to arouse audiences to a high
pitch of patriotic emotion. McCarthy knew the power
of television, and knew how to use it to dramatize
himself and his views, but he failed to consider that
television might be used against him.

Unlike the Radulovich program, which brought out

facts, the McCarthy program was a carefully edited attack. Murrow was able to do what no one else had done before because of the enormous reserve of credibility that he had with the American public. He was not an Ivy-league educated, big-city accented member of the press. He made his way into people's homes and won them over with his calm voice, his physical presence, and his care for life and the lives behind historic events. Murrow was a reporter with whom most Amercans felt very comfortable, and he made McCarthy look cheap and sleazy. The McCarthy program was calculated to show up the contrast between the two men. It might not have been "fair" television reporting, but it was probably the most effective program in the history of broadcasting.

5

I. F. Stone:

Digging out the Lies

The federal government in Washington spins out millions of words every day. There are thick reports from different agencies, testimony from hundreds of Congressional hearings, press releases from the president down to the Administrator in Charge of the Reclamation of Clams.

Who could possibly read all those words? Who can ever remember from one day to the next what was written yesterday? For over a quarter of a century it seemed to many people as if one man was reading and remembering. From 1953 until 1971, I. F. Stone ran one of the most unusual journalistic ventures in American history. With the help of his wife and an occasional assistant, he published a four-page weekly telling his readers what the government was saying and what it was doing.

I. F. Stone had a deceptively simple formula as a journalist. He filed away notes on what the politicians and bureaucrats said they were going to do—then he pulled out those notes when they did something else. It never upset him to call someone a liar, and he always told his readers who was lying and how.

"Now in the job of covering a capital," he once said, "there're really certain basic assumptions you have to operate on. The first is that every government is run by liars, and nothing they say should be believed. That's a prima facie assumption unless proven to the contrary."

It cost five dollars a year to get *I. F. Stone's Weekly* in the mail. His careful research and persistence in seeking facts made him one of the capital's most widely read journalists. Almost all reporters who cover Washington had their name on Izzy Stone's subscription list, as did the president, most congressmen, and thousands of bureaucrats. They might not like what they found in his newspaper, but they didn't want to miss whatever lie I. F. Stone might uncover. To thousands of other readers across the country, his weekly was where they could begin to make sense of the seemingly endless rainfall of news that filled the television news programs and the daily newspapers. Murray Kempton once said that the "average four-page issue of *I. F. Stone's Weekly* is more illuminating than the average Sunday edition of *The New York Times*."

I. F. Stone has always been considered a journalist of the left, but he has never been a predictable left-winger. He likes to call himself a "real radical, . . . not the bomb throwing stereotype, . . . but one who gets to the roots of the problems. My job . . . is to notice the things that most reporters overlook and to analyse those events from a radical point of view."

Politically, Stone is an eternal optimist. He is for-ever hoping that the system will deliver on its promises of a good society. In an article in *Ramparts*, Sol Stein points out that with each new presidential inaugura-tion, Stone comments about some omen of change for the better in the upcoming administration. No matter how many times I. F. Stone catches government offi-cials lying, no matter how many times he sees the military wasting lives, Stone simply refuses to give up hope. "I tell people to take the long view," says Stone. "Remember that when Moses came down from Mount Sinai, the race had advanced far enough by then that it was not necessary to have a commandment about cannibalism." It is this quality of hope that has made I. F. Stone an inspiration to his readers and to other journalists.

I. F. Stone was born in Haddonfield, New Jersey, in 1907. His parents were Russian immigrants. At age fourteen, he was already printing his own monthly, *The Progress*. At fifteen, he was covering his home-town for the local newspaper. He got a job with the

Philadelphia Inquirer while he was still in college, but he eventually dropped out of college because it was interfering with his work as a reporter. In the 1930s and 1940s he worked as a Washington correspondent for a series of liberal newspapers and magazines.

In 1952, the liberal paper he worked for folded. It was a tough time for a reporter with a radical reputation to be out of work. Joseph McCarthy had just been appointed head of the Senate Subcommittee on Investigations, the Korean War had whipped up hatred of Communists, and in death row in Sing Sing, Ethel and Julius Rosenberg, members of the American Communist Party, sat awaiting execution for treason in a case that is still being argued today.

I. F. Stone had $3500 severance pay from his last job. A friend loaned him $3000 more to try to put out his own newspaper. Stone says, "I had seen one experiment after another in liberal journalism go down to defeat. I thought the time had come to cut the cloth and try a paper so small and inexpensive it would pay for itself even in bad times." I. F. Stone decided that he would be the only reporter on his newspaper. His wife would handle the business end. He wouldn't even try to find advertisers. If enough people would pay $5 a year for a subscription, Stone figured he could pay for the printing and mailing, and still have enough to support his family.

In 1952, the problem was to find people willing to have a radical newsweekly delivered through the mail. McCarthyism and guilt by association were at their peak. People knew they could find themselves under suspicion just by subscribing to something like *I. F. Stone's Weekly*. Stone had lists from old liberal newspapers and other radical and liberal organizations from which he was gradually able to round up 5300 subscribers.

One of the early subscribers was labor organizer Al Bernstein, the father of Carl Bernstein, *The Washington Post* reporter. "In the early fifties," says Bernstein, "the witch hunters were so successful that the whole progressive movement went out of business. Really the only organ that I can recall in which you could get an objective view of what was really going on in the world was this four-page weekly of Izzie's."

Carl Bernstein grew up reading *I. F. Stone's Weekly* and believes that anybody who goes into what is known as investigative reporting, can't help but be influenced by Stone.

When Stone finally had enough subscribers to get started, he got an office in downtown Washington. He was used to working for fairly large organizations, and he had always assumed that a newspaper, no matter how small, needed an office. However, no one called the office with "hot" stories. In fact, nobody called at all, and the office became a drain on his meager financial resources.

When Stone started his weekly he had two main disadvantages. One was physical and the other political. The physical problem was that he had been going deaf since 1937. "As a result, I couldn't go to hearings and I got the habit of going around the next morning and reading the transcript myself. I soon discovered that if you went the next day and read it for yourself you always found things that reporters had missed, not because you were brighter, but because it's very hard to sit there all day and listen to a lot of stuff and catch it all."

Stone's second disadvantage was political, which he was able to turn into an advantage also. "I was starting in a very hostile atmosphere, and people didn't believe what I was saying, and I had no inside information. If I did nobody would believe it. I had to present my material in a form that was documented from the government's own sources."

After a few months, Stone gave up his office in downtown Washington and converted an upstairs bedroom in his home into an office where he still works today. The basement is filled with old newspapers and big alphabetical folders that hold Stone's main resource, his clippings. Stone is always planning on getting a truly systematic file system, but he never does.

Almost all of us read the paper and think, maybe I'll want this fact or that fact someday, but before we do anything about it, it's gone with the day's trash. Not so with Stone.

His day begins with the thud of newspapers arriving on his front porch at about 6:30 a.m.—*The Washington Post, The New York Times, The Baltimore Sun, The Wall Street Journal.* In the early morning hours, Stone ferrets through the newspapers and dozens of magazines, from *The Peking Review* to *Air Force and Space Digest.* Hundreds of tiny items get pushed into the huge folders. Later in the day, he may make a phone call about an item that intrigued him, or hike all over Washington in search of official documents.

For several years, particularly while McCarthyism was still strong, Stone was treated as a social and political pariah in Washington, something of an eccentric. For the first seven years of the *Weekly*'s existence, Stone was lucky to earn $125 a week after paying the expenses of the paper.

However, after the pall of McCarthyism lifted, the subscription list grew until the *Weekly* began to bring in a healthy income. Stone was able to send three children to Ivy League schools, and he likes to brag about the fact that he is a very successful capitalist. "It's really a solid enterprise run along good old-fashioned bourgeois lines," Stone once told a reporter for *Life* magazine. "It's the journalistic equivalent of the old-fashioned momma and poppa grocery store. My wife at one end of the table, and me at the other putting the paper out."

Stone enjoys tweaking the establishment about being the last successful capitalist, but a successful capitalist usually has to make compromises so that his product will sell, and this Stone has never done. Nothing in Stone's style of tone changed from the 1950s to the late 1960s. But in the sixties the political climate changed and Stone was not only socially and politically acceptable, but he became a hero. Stone is not particularly surprised by his new popularity. "I told my wife long ago," he once said at a speech, "I said, honey, I'm going to graduate from pariah to a character, and then if I last long enough I'll be regarded as a national institution. They'll say, 'Why, of course, it's a free country, look at Izzie . . . look at Izzie Stone.' "

The main reason for Stone's growing popularity was that so many people in the late 1960s came around to his way of thinking. Stone had always been at his best—his most persistent and incisive—when going after the military. He was one of the earliest critics of American involvement in Vietnam. He pointed out facts about Vietnam and the Vietnamese people, and showed the many ways the military was making incorrect assumptions.

One of Stone's most important stories was warning his readers that the official version of the Tonkin Gulf incident in Vietnam was not true. The United States claimed that its destroyers were outside North Vietnam's territorial limits, when suddenly they were attacked by North Vietnamese patrol boats. The United States destroyers hit back, sinking three North Vietnamese boats. No United States boats were sunk and there were no injuries to United States citizens.

President Johnson treated this incident as a major crisis, an attack almost as infamous as Pearl Harbor. He went on television and in a grave voice said, "Aggression, deliberate, willful, and systematic aggression has unmasked its face to the entire world. The world remembers; the world must never forget that aggression unchallenged is aggression unleashed." In order to check North Vietnam's unleashed aggression, President Johnson asked Congress to grant him the authority to take whatever steps necessary to demonstrate to North Vietnam that it could not attack our ships and get away with it.

All the newspapers across the country accepted the government's version of the Tonkin Gulf incident, particularly the claim that the attack was unprovoked. The press backed up the president's claim that *we* had been attacked and *we* were the victims.

Only in *I. F. Stone's Weekly* was it suggested that

perhaps the attack had not been unprovoked and that perhaps the United States was not the victim. All I. F. Stone did was to read closely the published accounts of the debate in the Senate. Senator Wayne Morse, one of the two senators to vote against the resolution, submitted evidence that there was a legitimate disagreement between the North Vietnamese and us over exactly where their territorial water began. Further, Morse brought up the fact that the North Vietnamese had been attacked just days before by South Vietnamese vessels supplied by the United States. The fact that our destroyers were patrolling the area could easily be seen as an act of provocation by the North Vietnamese. If Cuban patrol boats, made in the USSR, attacked the coast of Florida, and huge Russian destroyers sat nearby, offering protection to the Cubans, we would undoubtedly think that the Russians were provoking us, and that we were justified in attacking.

Years later, it was learned that I. F. Stone was right. President Johnson had been convinced that the only way to help the South Vietnamese win was to have American bombers attack the North. The problem was that we were not at war with North Vietnam, and Johnson doubted that he could get Congress to go along with the two-thirds majority needed to declare war. He was looking for a way to get a resolution allowing him to widen the war. The Tonkin Gulf incident gave him the opportunity he needed. The general press was so caught up with the patriotism of the moment that they did not report Wayne Morse's objections that the incident was provoked, and the incident wasn't investigated until the late 1960s. The Pentagon papers revealed that President Johnson and his top military aides had for a long time planned bombing raids on the North, and were just waiting for an excuse to give the American people as to why we were bombing a people we were not at war with. After the Pentagon papers were published, reporters started to interview sailors who had served on the destroyers, and many of the sailors confirmed I. F. Stone's suspicion that they had never been attacked at all.

However, Stone published his suspicions about the Tonkin Gulf incident itself. He was the only reporter in Washington to catch the truth in the story. "What I suspected about the Tonkin Gulf," Stone had said, "and what I showed in my little paper within a week, anybody else in town could have done. All you had to do was to first read the wire services very carefully, and then read carefully the testimony taken by the Senate Foreign Relations Committee, and then begin asking a few more questions. It was very clear that something was amiss."

There it is again, the reporter's feeling that some-

thing is "amiss." Then digging for the facts to find out
if the facts prove that your feeling is right. A few
years ago, Stone was honored by a group of young
reporters who called themselves "counter-journalists."
In his speech accepting their honor, Stone said, "I tell
you I really have so much fun, I ought to be arrested.
Sometimes I feel like a small boy covering a hell of a
big fire. It's just wonderful and exciting, and you're
a cub reporter and god had given you a big fire to
cover. And you forget that it's really burning."

I. F. Stone is important because he has never really
forgotten that it's a "real fire" he's covering. Every
injustice hidden in the dry figures of the budget truly
upsets him. Every bomb we drop without justification
outrages him. But he never gives up. In December
1971, after he turned 64, Stone said he was getting
tired. He decided to stop publishing his weekly and
to concentrate on doing long pieces of journalism for
The New York Review of Books. His output has hardly
slowed down.

6

Gail Sheehy:

Reporting on Prostitution

Gail Sheehy is a reporter who believes in immersing herself thoroughly in her story, a method she describes as "total saturation." When she became curious about the increase in prostitution in the United States in the late 1960s and early 1970s, she found herself spending the next two years of her life trailing after prostitutes in New York City in order to present an authentic account of prostitutes and prostitution.

It turned out to be a dangerous assignment. Sheehy admitted that she was scared almost all of the time she was with prostitutes. "I never spent more than one hour in any one 'pross' hotel," she said. "The people in them are often psychotic and you never know when you are going to be knifed."

There is very little in Gail Sheehy's background that would indicate that she would be willing to take

risks to learn everything she could about prostitution.
She was brought up in a conventional middle-class
home in Mamaroneck, New York. She graduated from
the Univerity of Vermont and became a traveling
home economist for the J.C. Penney Company, and
later a fashion coordinator in a department store.

She broke into journalism as a fashion editor for
the *Rochester (N.Y.) Democrat & Chronicle.* Eventually she came to New York City and got a job as a
feature writer for *The New York Herald Tribune.*
When *The Tribune* went out of business, Sheehy became a free-lance writer, doing most of her articles
for *New York Magazine* where almost all of her articles on prostitution first appeared.

In writing about prostitution, Sheehy tried to show
a link between women's liberation and the increase in
prostitution. She has stated that she is neither a doc-
trinaire feminist nor a new journalist, but that she
thinks of herself as a questioning feminist and an experimental writer.

Sheehy's unique style of covering a story combines
reporting with experimental writing, and is quite different from the technique of the other writers in this
book. Oriana Fallaci might use some of the techniques
of new journalism, but when she interviews someone,
the reader trusts that she is reporting accurately, and
the reader always knows exactly who it is that Fallaci
is quoting.

Sheehy takes greater liberties with her sources. In order to achieve what she calls "total saturation," Sheehy uses many techniques more often associated with fiction writing than with reporting. For example, in an article about the daily life of streetwalkers, Sheehy told the story of a prostitute called "Redpants" and her pimp, "Sugarman." The article is full of details concerning what Redpants thinks about, how she dresses, and how she lives.

Sheehy writes vividly about the thrills that Redpants gets from her work, and Sheehy makes her reader feel as if he knows how Redpants thinks. "It gets in the blood," Sheehy writes. "All night long peeping and hiding, zipping and fastening. Hustling bucks and ducking the third division boys . . . those earnest young plainclothesmen assigned to the vice squad. The pace itself, the sheer velocity of risk is a drug. And then a girl controls the situation with her tricks. She sets the price and delivers the pleasure or doesn't . . . pretending submission while all the time she is in control.

Despite the ring of authenticity that the articles have, after they appeared Sheehy admitted that "Redpants" was not exactly real. There was a prostitute named "Redpants," but Sheehy hardly talked to her, much less knew the intimate details of Redpants' life that had been presented in the article. Sheehy used Redpants' name and put together a story out of bits and pieces of material she had collected about several prostitutes. In short, Sheehy had created the sort of person she imagined Redpants to be.

The point of journalism as opposed to fiction is that the reader trusts that the material is based on fact. Sheehy's technique was widely criticized for disguising fiction as journalism. Sheehy responded to this criticism by protesting that all the information in the article was real and that in order to pull all her months of reporting into a unified story, she had used the character of Redpants, who was a composite of several different girls at various stages of their involvement in prostitution. In defending herself, Sheehy insisted that every word of the article was true, and that it was based on police cases, interviews, personal observations and experiences.

Sheehy further explained that she had to write the story that way because it was impossible to get to know any one prostitute very well since their work is illegal and they are very suspicious and distrustful of what they call "straight" women. Furthermore, she found it very difficult to find any prostitute who would talk to her, much less pour out her life story.

To begin her research on prostitution, Sheehy went out on the street to observe the girls at work. She even dressed for the part in a tight sweater and tight pants. Every night she went out during the streetwalkers working hours: 6 p.m. to 4 a.m. She had to learn the rhythm and habits of the prostitutes, and to recognize regular faces. Her brother-in-law played the role of her "John" (the man buying a prostitute's favors) and he learned how much the girls got for turning a "trick." Sheehy and her brother-in-law followed the prostitutes and their Johns into hotels and even registered themselves into the hotel. Sheehy reports that during this stage of her work she ate badly, developed blisters and soon felt as degraded and defensive as any of the hustlers she was trying to describe.

During the day, Sheehy talked to everyone who might know anything about prostitutes. She interviewed police commanders and assistant district attorneys. She talked to the large group of lawyers who make their money from representing prostitutes, and they told her many first-hand stories about the lives of their clients.

Still Sheehy could find no way to get to the prostitutes directly. When she approached them on the street, asking them to grant her an interview, they laughed at her and refused. Finally, Sheehy became friendly with "Bobby," the doorman at the Waldorf Hotel in New York City. Bobby was trusted by many of the prostitutes who considered him as a kind man who cared about them. Bobby introduced Sheehy to some of the prostitutes who were his friends and tried to convince the girls that Sheehy could be trusted. It was Bobby who eventually introduced Sheehy to "Redpants," and Sheehy was even able to make an appointment with her. But the night before the interview was to take place, Redpants told Sheehy she wouldn't come because the other girls on the street had threatened to cut her up if she talked.

Despite the difficulty of finding prostitutes to give her interviews, Sheehy stuck with the story, and gradually accumulated much knowledge about prostitution. It was then that she decided to write her article as if it were about the life of one prostitute when, in actuality, it was about many. While many journalists severely criticized the article, the prostitutes who read it were impressed. Many believed that Sheehy was the first to accurately portray their lives. After the article was published several prostitutes decided Sheehy could be trusted and they began to talk to her at length concerning some of their deepest feelings about their work. One prostitute even allowed Sheehy to stash her tape recorder under a bed in order to monitor what a prostitute said to her "John."

Despite this vote of confidence from her actual sources, many readers are made uneasy by Sheehy's techniques. The vivid quality of her writing, the piling of detail upon detail is convincing, and yet the reader is never quite certain that things happened in exactly the way Sheehy describes. This leaves a nagging doubt in many readers' minds.

In another article about a celebrated New York

pimp named David, Sheehy compressed several weeks of David's life into twenty-four hours. The reader thinks Sheehy is reporting an actual day and night in the life of a pimp, and it is a breathtaking report because the pimp never seems to stop. He is pictured as David the Dynamo, always hustling.

"Be warned," Sheehy writes. "David is the juggler always balancing the forces of will and desire . . . working out the combinations of weakness in those around him . . . until their bodies become his possession. David can think of more ways to extract money in less time than a ball takes to arc the juggler's head."

Sheehy arranged the details of the article to deliberately give the reader the feeling that everything is taking place in an exact order—and all in one day. The day starts with David trying to recruit a pretty young girl into the business. And then it is mid-afternoon. A few pages later, a heading in the article reads "11:00 p.m." The reader cannot help getting the impression that it is the same night. The girl arrives at David's apartment.

As the chapter continues, Sheehy constantly makes the reader aware of the passage of time.

12:30 p.m. Two of David's prostitutes arrive

2:00 a.m. David escorts the prostitutes to a stockbroker's party

11:00 a.m. The next morning. David is back at his
apartment. He is on the telephone, hustling up
more work for his "girls."

The article successfully gives the reader a sense of
both the decadence and energetic quality of the life
David leads. However, the truth is that the day and
night and the next morning did not happen the way
Sheehy describes it. Sheehy took incidents she observed
from weeks of following David around and wove them
into a "typical" day. Sheehy counters criticism of this
technique with the same argument she made about the
Redpants incident—that every incident in the chapter
is true and she is simply using dramatic license to pull
the chapter together. In the articles on David and
Redpants, it certainly seems that the details are
accurate. The reader is left convinced that such people
as Redpants and David do exist.

However, in another article entitled "The Ultimate
Trick," her composite character seems less believable.
The article is about women who are the companions
and wives of rich and famous men, and Sheehy argues
that these women are simply prostitutes on a grand
scale. The lead character in the article is a widow of
a very rich, old millionaire. The story takes place on
the day of the millionaire's funeral. Again, the character is not real, nor is the situation. It is another

composite character which Sheehy says was assembled from "several women, rich courtesans, whose quotes, anecdotes and supporting cast are assembled from several years of acquaintance with their lives." Unfortunately, the article reads much more like bad fiction than journalism.

Nothing in this article rings true. All the characters seem exaggerated and the events melodramatic. The widow is described as "not fat, but overripe." Her eyes "rove possessively." The widow drifts in a "particularly dreamlike state." Sheehy describes the chauffeur driving the widow around the estate and makes up a conversation. " 'It's hard to find a man,' " Sheehy has the widow say out loud. " 'Not if you're looking for a real man,' the chauffer said, letting his breath come hard."

It is writing like this that makes the article resemble a paperback romance or even a true-love comic book more than journalism.

If Sheehy were only trying to be an experimental journalist parts of her work might be regarded as rather unsuccessful. However, there is another aspect to Sheehy's work, and this other aspect makes her a top-rate investigative reporter. Sheehy's stories on prostitution do not merely give the details of the life of the prostitute, but expose prostitution as a very lucrative and big business. Furthermore, in writing her story she was able to uncover the names of some very influential people who were indirectly profiting from prostitution.

Using the most current figures available there are between 200,000 and 250,000 prostitutes in the United States. Sheehy found that most prostitutes turn at least six tricks a day. Using the bottom price of about $20 a trick, prostitution turns over the incredible sum of between seven and nine billion dollars a year, and none of it is taxed.

The prostitutes keep very little of the money they earn themselves. Often all of it goes to their pimp, who simply buys wigs and clothes for the prostitutes, and gives them a place to live when they are not hustling. Most prostitutes start out in their teens, but by the time they are thirty, it is difficult for them to continue to earn a living by hustling. Furthermore, because prostitution is a criminal offense, most girls are saddled with a police record which makes it almost impossible to find another job once they are too old to be prostitutes.

As part of her research Sheehy spent weeks with the police as they patroled the streets picking up girls. Because the girls are rarely caught in the act of making a specific proposal for a specific price, most prostitutes are picked up on the charge of loitering. Ninety percent of the loitering cases are dismissed. However, the girls are left with a permanent arrest record, and they or their pimps have to pay for the lawyer. Even girls who are found guilty of the more serious crime of making a proposal to a plainclothes policeman are rarely jailed. Their lawyers usually convince the judges to let them go for a $25 to $50 fine and give them a week to pay. The judges are reluctant to jail the girls because (1) there are so many of them and (2) no one has been hurt.

Prostitution is often called a "victimless crime" because the prostitute doesn't hurt anyone. There have been many arguments that prostitution should be made legal, but Sheehy strongly argues that prostitution is not an innocent business.

She points out that in 1933 when the repeal of prohibition forced the Mafia to think of new ways to make money, they became involved in the prostitution business. Sheehy claims the Mafia is involved in more than prostitution, and that they control pornography shops and peep shows that crop up wherever prostitutes abound. "The one thing prostitution is *not*," argues Sheehy, "is a victimless crime. It attracts a wide species of preying criminals and generates a long line of victims, beginning with the most obvious and least understood—the prostitute herself."

Sheehy attempts to show a link between prostitution, violence, and crime. She discovered that the working prostitutes were turning more and more to violence.

"They work on their backs as little as possible," she
writes. "The bulk of their business is not the dispensa-
tion of pleasure. It is to swindle, mug, rob, knife, and
possibly even murder their patrons."

Petty crimes have always been associated with prostitution, but Sheehy discovered that in the past few
years, New York's prostitutes have manifested a growing incidence of violence. Sheehy suggests that there
is a link between women's liberation and the violence
of the prostitutes. She argues that women's liberation
had caused the prostitute to realize that men go about
crime much more directly, and that prostitutes might
follow their example. "Why give one's body," Sheehy
asks, "when it's so much easier to just attack the cus-
tomer, take his money and be done with it?"

Shortly before she began investigating prostitution,
Sheehy had a fellowship to study at Colombia University under Margaret Mead. One of Mead's theories
is that women are potentially more violent than men
once they shed their traditional passive role. Mead
believes that men and male animals fight for many
reasons, and they do not always fight to kill. They
often fight as a game, to show off their prowess and
to impress females. They have rules which often stop
them from killing their opponent. Women, on the
other hand, according to Mead, have no built-in inhibi-
tions against killing. When they do fight, they fight

much fiercer than men and there is no game about it. They fight to kill.

Sheehy was very impressed with Mead's arguments, and she used her study of prostitutes to test Mead's theories. In 1970, just before Sheehy started her articles, there was a sudden outbreak of violence involving prostitutes. In one month, a visiting Italian manufacturer was stabbed to death outside the Hilton Hotel by a prostitute. The former defense minister of West Germany, a large muscular man, was mugged and robbed in a car outside the Plaza Hotel. Charles Adams, the cartoonist, was followed by a group of prostitutes offering him their business. He ignored them and refused to turn around. The prostitutes splashed burning acid on the back of his head.

As Sheehy investigated the link between violence and prostitutes, she discovered that women in general had suddenly turned to violent crimes. The FBI statistics for the 1960s showed that female arrests for major crimes rose 156.2 percent. For women under eighteen, the rate of participation in violent crimes—"murder, robbery, and aggravated assault"—was up 230 percent.

Sheehy believes that there is a new violent edge to women in America, that women are choosing violence as a way of life. "I decided [the subculture of prostitution] was the place to pick up the warning signals.

. . . Violent women are part of a much larger cultural shift," she writes.

But Sheehy never quite proves her theory. The reader is left confused about exactly how prostitutes, violence, and women's liberation are linked together. It is only when she turns to investigating exactly who makes money from prostitution, that the confusion in Sheehy's writing disappears. There was one aspect of prostitution that was almost totally ignored until Sheehy began her work: the landlords. Before her investigation, no one had asked about the owners of the hotels which so many prostitutes frequented.

It took Sheehy six months of research to find out the facts. She had to go from one city department to another trying to track down tax records. She had to learn accounting in order to make her way through the dummy corporations and other ruses used to hide the real owners of the prostitution hotels. Finally she was able to publish a list.

The article caused quite a sensation. The names of people collecting profit from hotels where prostitution was practiced were some of the most respected names in New York real estate. Several were members of the city's Times Square Development Council, an organization designed to rid the Times Square area of prostitution. Some landlords on this council were raking in a healthy profit from the very hotels they were publicly saying they wanted to put out of business.

Sheehy went to interview the landlords on her list, and she wrote that at the outset of every interview each landlord claimed that he didn't really own the particular prostitution hotel that Sheehy claimed he did. Only after Sheehy brought out her documentation did the landlord admit that it was his property. At this point in the interview, each landlord protested that they were trying to sell the hotel. Sheehy pointed out, however, that the prostitution hotels and massage parlors pay high rent and bring in a good income.

Sheehy's articles on prostitution-hotel landlords caused the mayor of the City of New York to try to do something about making the landlords clean up their properties. He called Sheehy and congratulated her on her articles, and invited her to meet with his chief corporation counsel. After some research, the city's lawyers discovered that they had already had a law on their books that made the landlords responsible if their property was being used illegally.

Of all her articles dealing with prostitution, the article on landlords was Sheehy's best. It put her directly in the tradition of Lincoln Steffens and Upton Sinclair, the muckrakers who not only pointed out corruption, but took an active part in trying to bring about reform.

Sheehy is a hardworking reporter, who can go after elusive facts and pin them down. She can present them in a logical manner, as she did in her article on land-lords. However, if there is one complaint about Sheehy, it is that she tries to do too much. She tries to be muckraker, new journalist, sociologist, and novelist all at once, and it doesn't always work.

Currently she seems to be moving in the direction of concentration on sociology and psychology, as she has begun an extensive study of the different stages of adult life. A few of these articles have already appeared. They present the new idea that adults go through changes every ten years that are as distinct as the changes that occur between childhood and adolescence.

Once again these articles have caused controversy and a lot of discussion among journalists. The idea that she is presenting fascinates many people but still no one is exactly sure where she is getting her facts. No matter what she does, she is almost always an interesting journalist whose work will always cause arguments and force other journalists to reevaluate their own styles.

Bibliography

BERNSTEIN, CARL, AND WOODWARD, BOB. *All the President's Men.* New York: Simon and Schuster, 1974.

FALLACI, ORIANA. *The Egoists: Sixteen Surprising Interviews.* Chicago: H. Regnery, 1968.

————. *If the Sun Dies.* Translated by Pamela Swinglehurst. New York: Atheneum, 1966.

FRIENDLY, FRED. *Due to Circumstances beyond Our Control.* New York: Random House, 1967.

KENDRICK, ALEXANDER. *Prime Time: The Life of Edward R. Murrow.* Boston: Little, Brown and Company, 1969.

MURROW, EDWARD R. *In Search of Light: The Broadcasts of Edward R. Murrow, 1938–1961.* Edited by Edward Bliss. New York: Alfred A. Knopf, 1967.

SHEEHY, GAIL. *Hustling: Prostitution in Our Wide Open Society.* New York: Delacorte Press, 1973.

―――. *Panthermania: The Clash of Black Against Black in One American City.* New York: Harper & Row, 1971.

STONE, ISIDOR F. *The Haunted Fifties.* New York: Random House, 1963.

―――. *The I. F. Stone Weekly Reader.* Edited by Neil Middleton. New York: Random House, 1973.

―――. *In Time of Torment.* New York: Random House, 1967.

―――. *The Killings at Kent State: How Murder Went Unpunished.* New York: Vintage Books, 1971.

―――. *Polemics and Prophecies, 1967–1970.* New York: Random House, 1970.

FURTHER READINGS IN
INVESTIGATIVE JOURNALISM

CROUSE, TIMOTHY. *The Boys on the Bus.* New York: Random House, 1973.

THE WASHINGTON POST WRITERS GROUP. *Of the Press, for the Press, by the Press (& Others, too)*. Edited by Laura Longley Babb. New York: Dell, 1974.

WOLFE, TOM. *The New Journalism*. New York: Harper & Row, 1973.

Index